THE
RENAISSANCE
SOCIETY

HOW THE SHIFT FROM DREAM SOCIETY
TO THE AGE OF INDIVIDUAL CONTROL
WILL CHANGE THE WAY YOU DO BUSINESS

ROLF JENSEN
MIKA AALTONEN

New York Chicago San Francisco Lisbon London Madrid Mexico City
Milan New Delhi San Juan Seoul Singapore Sydney Toronto

1 2 3 4 5 6 7 8 9 0   DOC/DOC   1 9 8 7 6 5 4 3

ISBN   978-0-07-180605-3
MHID   0-07-180605-9

e-ISBN 978-0-07-180606-0
e-MHID   0-07-180606-7

McGraw-Hill books are available at special quantity discounts to use as premiums and sales promotions or for use in corporate training programs. To contact a representative, please e-mail us at bulksales@mcgraw-hill.com.

This book is printed on acid-free paper.

Library of Congress Cataloging-in-Publication Data

Jensen, Rolf.
    The renaissance society : how the shift from dream society to the age of individual control will change the way you do business / by Rolf Jensen and Mika Aaltonen.
        pages cm
    Includes bibliographical references and index.
    ISBN 978-0-07-180605-3 (alk. paper) -- ISBN 0-07-180605-9 (alk. paper)
    1. Business forecasting.   2. Twenty-first century--Forecasts.   3. Civilization, Modern.   I. Aaltonen, Mika.   II. Title.
    HD30.27.J476 2013
    338.501'12--dc23

                                                                    2013002281

To all those people, whatever their official position, who give rise to the new Renaissance.

Contents

Preface

THESE ARE DIFFICULT TIMES, BUT THEN AGAIN, DIFFICULT times are not an exception in our history. The early years of the 1400s did not look promising for Europeans. The bubonic plague had returned to every generation after its arrival in 1348, with a devastating outbreak in 1400 to 1401. The Roman Empire was split with a bitter leadership crisis, with one emperor deposed, another murdered, and a third deserted by his army. Finally, the papacy was split between Rome and Avignon in one of the saddest chapters in the history of the Church.

Yet, these were the times that gave rise to the Renaissance. While not totally forgetting medieval imperatives for salvation and God's teachings, shifting the goals of human knowledge and rejecting superstition gave room for new science, new societies and, if you wish—the New World was created.

But this is not a book about history. This is a book about the future—the future of companies, the marketplace, and society. Future studies is not an exact science. We cannot prove what the future will be, but we have to try to determine it, since the decisions we make today are based on our assumptions about the future. So, as leaders, we need to be prepared in the best way possible. You should read this book not as a blueprint for

the years ahead, but for inspiration. Join us and explore the future as it rises above the horizon and eventually comes to us as the present. We want to welcome the future as a good friend that we wish to meet, not as an enemy that we hope to avoid. The future is a most exciting and rewarding place to visit.

Four basic ideas have guided our work:

1. A business book on the future must be global in order to reflect reality, today's and especially tomorrow's.
2. Nobody can be sure about trends and developments. There is no "Master of the Universe." In an interconnected world, things are too complicated. So, we should invite the reader to reflect, get inspired, and draw his own conclusions.
3. This is not a book predicting doom and gloom. We are about to leave a prolonged economic crisis, and this is the right time to rethink our business models. A crisis is both a problem and an opportunity. We focus more on opportunities.
4. Rolf Jensen's bestseller *The Dream Society* was published by McGraw-Hill in 1999. It was a book about the future of the mature economies, and it introduced the experience economy—the emotion-driven marketplace. *The Renaissance Society* is a sequel in the sense that it updates the trends discussed in the first book, but it differs because it is a global book and because of the long time horizon. It is not an update of the dream society; it is a *new* dream society.

Out of these guiding ideas and with immense research and analysis, we were able to draw three clear, distinct, but interconnected scenarios.

The first one—The Renaissance Society—is, in our opinion, the strongest one, and the reason why we named the book accordingly. It is based on how different trends, ideas, needs, and challenges come together, pointing in the same direction. Just as in the first Renaissance dating back 600 years to northern Italy, the Renaissance Society renounces the existing organizing principles of the industrial society that are based on top-down management, hierarchy, and control. When this is done, new energy and hope is released, and people will start to and be able to reorganize themselves from the bottom-up in their daily practices and communities.

The second one—The Green Society—is, in our opinion, a necessity. Again, there are several reasons and trends presented in the book that call for more sustainable ways of living, working, and consuming. Thus, ultimately, societies that destroy their environments, destroy themselves.

The third scenario—The Risk Society—benefits, just like the Renaissance Society, from the technological developments that push the limits of knowledge further, but takes advantage of them within the industrial mindset, thus aiming at increasing control and supervision.

The book represents a collaborative effort between Rolf and Mika, and we are both responsible for the words. However, we want to thank a lot of people for inspiration and for making us go "the extra mile." You will find the names and organizations in the endnotes. On a personal note, however, there are several people that we wish to thank.

To Rolf's wife, Birgitte, and their son, Klaus, thank you for your tireless encouragement and help. Thank you to Dream Company's board for your strong belief in the project.

To Mika's wife, Susanna, and their son, Anton, thank you for your patience and support.

Thank you also to the editors at McGraw-Hill, Pattie Amoroso, Donya Dickerson, and Mary Glenn, who really improved the manuscript.

Rolf Jensen

Mika Aaltonen

The Reader's Manual

EACH CHAPTER OF THIS BOOK CAN BE READ SEPARATELY. WE know that most people don't have the time to read a book from cover to cover in one day. Which chapter should you read first? This manual may be of help.

The Introduction, "Setting the Scene," presents the 12 main challenges that are facing companies today. It is a summary of most of the ideas in the rest of the book, and it gives you a good taste of what to expect. The conclusion at the end of the book, Chapter 7, can be read separately. It is the authors' discussion of the big picture. We suggest that the many changes in Western societies could point toward an upheaval, or even a revolution. The most likely scenario is an exciting one, "the second Renaissance," and it would entail new ideas in art, business, and science—ideas that are coming from below, from you and me.

Chapter 1 is a comprehensive overview of the material world, the world of money and stuff. It provides a view of the global distribution of wealth and poverty, both now and in 30 years' time. It analyzes the new multipolar world and the growth of cities. In a digitalized world, cybersecurity becomes increasingly vital. Chapter 2 is an overview of the nonmaterial world: our values, cultures, and habits. These changes will open new

markets, such as the "I do exist" market and the happiness market. Together, the two chapters present (with a lot of figures) an idea of what the years ahead will be like, and at the same time examine numerous new market trends. Chapter 3 looks at the interaction between production and consumption when new technology is introduced. The one-person factory is just one example. Chapter 4 addresses the developments in what may become the world's largest industry, learning. Chapter 5 views the globe as one interconnected system and discusses the need for a sustainable future. Chapter 6 claims that management is not a progressive science, but is about almost eternal dilemmas.

We have written about ideas and trends that already are above the horizon, but we did not limit ourselves to them. Most of this material is breaking new ground, like the chapters on learning and systems. As mentioned earlier, our aim is to inspire the reader—to get her as excited about the future as we are. We wish to put a spotlight on the path into the future. Reading this may be fun, but an assessment of the future business environment is the raw material, the starting point for any discussion of visions and strategy. This applies to both private and public companies, and it is vital in our own lives.

Remember, the future is where you will spend the rest of your life!

Introduction

Setting the Scene

ALL SUCCESSFUL VISIONS AND STRATEGIES ARE BASED ON A solid assessment of how markets will develop, both in the near term and in the long term. No strategy is better than your idea of the business environment. The book provides an overview of markets and opportunities, both in the United States and globally. The trends presented here are intended as an inspiration for your visions and strategies. We strongly believe that any important change or innovation in your company must begin with the future: what will it look like? The answer is the starting point for the strategy process because the future is an eternal source of inspiration—especially in times of crisis and big changes.

"Setting the Scene" has not distilled all the trends discussed in the book, but focuses on those that are of special relevance to American companies and institutions. We are trying to address the crucial question: if you want to welcome the future as a good friend (and not as an enemy!), what should your company or organization do now? We have summarized the trends in 12 brief points.

THE EXTENDED NOW

In a static world, there is no need to study the future—it will be the same as today. The need to study the future increases as the world becomes more dynamic, with more and more agents of change shaping the market. The future will not be like the present. The best way to discover change is to use the principle of the "extended now." Consider the present to be the next 10 to 15 years. This is the opposite of the current thinking in the West—in particular, in politics and business in the United States. Short-termism rules—not in all companies, but in most. That prevents a proper study of the future. A perspective is needed; if you are concerned only with the next quarter, you are losing sight of important trends.

The extended now provides the perspective; it makes you stand back and discover the trends that are invisible in the short term. Successful Asian companies base their investments and strategies on the extended now. Fashions in management are always based on what works, and this works for most Chinese companies. Will Western companies find inspiration from Asia? From short-termism to the extended present is a fundamental change in the logic of politics and in business. It may take time, but if you start now, a world of opportunities and ideas for your company will emerge.

THE WEST IS BETWEEN DREAMS

The West (the United States and the other mature economies) is in crisis, and GDP growth has been low for many years. The East (the emerging economies), by contrast, is growing fast—actually twice as fast or more. Will this situation continue for

years to come? The East is pursuing a material dream: cars, travel, fashion, a house. The ordinary people are working hard to fulfill their dream, and they are doing so in harmony with their governments; for example, nearly 90 percent of Chinese say that they trust their government. After decades in which ideologies were put ahead of economic growth, this is not surprising—enthusiasm has been unleashed, with remarkable results.

In most Western countries, the material dream has been fulfilled for a lot of people; their dream has faded. Remember, economic growth is created not by governments, but by people—by you and me. According to Gallup, in the United States, many people are dissatisfied with the country's direction (only 40 percent are satisfied now; in 1965, the percentage was 80 percent). In addition, 55 percent of Americans think it is unlikely that young people will have a better life than their parents. The West is between dreams, between the material dream and whatever the next one will be. High growth rates in the mature economies are a possibility, but only if people in these economies discover a new dream. This must be a dream that inspires the majority, just as the material dream did in the 1950s and earlier, when it was strong in the United States.

What kind of dream will this be? One possibility is a second Renaissance, a setting free of ideas and innovation, just as the first Renaissance in Europe 600 years ago set ordinary people free from the iron grip of authorities. They could act on their own (and they did) in science, arts, and exploring the globe. A new Renaissance will not stem from some ideology, but from individual people who will inspire the many. Will this be a revolution? No, but it will be about bypassing the established authorities. It will produce a flatter society with less belief in authority. Renaissance means "to be reborn, to renew."

THE THIRD INDUSTRIAL REVOLUTION

The first Industrial Revolution happened in the United Kingdom. It involved factories powered by steam or water. The second Industrial Revolution happened in the United States; it involved the assembly line. The third Industrial Revolution will happen during the next 10 years. It will be based on nanotechnology and the 3D printer, which prints in three dimensions. The 3D printer produces one-of-a-kind products or a limited number of copies. It is perfectly suited to the era of individualization. The one-person factory with a few printers will open up possibilities for a lot of young entrepreneurs. They can produce works of art, but also bicycles or even helicopters. This third Industrial Revolution may prove to be the most important of the three. Many people will leave their factory jobs and start their own businesses. You will discover this trend if your horizon is the extended now. If you study only the short term, you will discover only centralization and automation.

THE 2018 RECESSION

The current recession is fading in most Western countries, but the economic crisis is still on, and it will last longer than usual in the mature economies, including the United States. The timing, however, fits nicely into the pattern of economic history. If we study government statistics on the recurring recessions in the United States, we find that, on average, a recession occurs every six years. Therefore, the next recession will happen in 2018 if growth begins in 2012 or 2013. Can we trust history and statistics? Yes, we can; the recession may happen a bit earlier or a bit later than this, but it will happen. Don't listen to all

the clever people who say, "This time it is different." It is not. Recessions are in the lifeblood of the financial markets; they have come with a disturbing regularity for the past 100 years and more. The extended now is again our helper in assessing the future. Will governments act to prevent the next recession? If we believe history (and there is every reason to do so), they will not; it will come as a surprise, just as it did this time, and just as it has done every time. For a company, preparing may be a clever move, but what is more likely to happen is that most companies will not avoid the "surprise."

THE FLAT SOCIETY

In 2012, when asked by Gallup, more than 40 percent of U.S. voters considered themselves to be "independent," up from 28 percent in 2004. The same thing is happening in Europe; people are leaving the mass parties, the mass movements, the unions, and the established church. We don't believe in authority; we think of ourselves as independent human beings. We make our own decisions; we don't buy the set menu; our views and our values are formed "à la carte"—that is, we follow our own ideas. It's an individualized society, and one that is more difficult to manage from above, but the result is a richer and more diverse society. This is bad news for the establishment, but good news for the individual. Decreasing belief in authority is a long-term trend, long but stable. We are approaching the flat society, with flatter hierarchies both in society and in companies. This is the result of education and better access to social media. When you are managing individuals, not big groups of people, decision making must be decentralized. Voters and employees will feel empowered;

leaders will have to adapt or leave. The trend augurs a richer society, with more ideas, more values, and more opportunities. It is a trend for the long term and it is global (remember the Arab Spring), and we must ask: what comes after democracy? The answer is a decentralized democracy with more choices for each citizen. It may be a hard lesson for politicians who were educated in the past, but they will have to adjust to the flat society.

THE TWENTY-FIRST-CENTURY GROWTH INDUSTRIES

In the United States and other mature economies, 75 percent of GDP comes from services; just 25 percent comes from manufacturing, industry, and agriculture combined. The future belongs to services. Imagine the U.S. economy as being completely dominated by services (95 percent); it will happen some time during this century, largely because of automation. We must ask: what industries will dominate? The answer is that the most likely growth industries are health services and learning. Health services are partly public and partly private, but you can expect them to become both privatized and globalized in most countries. As nations already use approximately 10 percent of GDP on healthcare, we have a new world industry. Which country or company will dominate in 10 to 15 years? A competition that is just as fierce as the one that is happening now in car production (the East versus the West) will take place. Learning is mostly within the public sector, but you can expect it to gradually become privatized. This has begun with educational games—software that helps students in schools and universities learn more and faster. There is a

looming learning revolution. Perhaps "Disney Learning" and "Pixar Learning" will play an important part, combining fun, experiences, and learning. Again, we must expect an East-West competition. It may take some time because of the different languages involved (translations will be needed), but some educational programs may not need words at all.

MENTAL ILLNESSES

Most experts find that around 25 percent of the populations in the West suffer from a diagnosable mental illness during any given year. All of us probably know some family member, friend, or colleague who has a mental problem, whether it is talked about or not. It is assumed that the percentage is the same in the East. On top of that, there are minor or periodic depressions and stress. This is a golden opportunity for forward-looking companies. The market is still in its infancy, but when we allow ourselves to talk openly about mental illnesses and when new cures are discovered, it is possible that the market for curing mental illnesses will equal that for curing somatic illnesses. This will not happen soon, but it will happen in 10 to 15 years. The law of the extended now applies here, since there is a prize to be won for the first mover.

THE STORE AS THEATER

Worldwide, more than a billion people have bought some product online, and the figure is growing by more than 10 percent each year. This is, of course, a challenge to stores and retail chains. They will have to be able to sell both online and offline,

and most of them are doing that already. Offline and online, yes, it has to be done. The important trend is not adapting to the Internet, it is the changing habits of the consumer.

In the old days, you went to buy shoes when you needed them. It was as simple as that. Nowadays, you buy shoes to address the question: "Who am I? Whom do I want to become?" Our products constitute "who we are" and whether we belong to this or that group. That is why the old-fashioned store must upgrade its sales clerks to casters. The store will become the theater of the future. When you want to change the way you present yourself to the world (in a small or large way), you will go to the casters. However, there will be a difference: in the theater, you have to fit into certain roles, whereas in the store theater, all kind of roles will be open to you. When the stores are transformed into theaters, the retail industry will regain its attraction to young people—it will be seen as an exciting growth industry with ample room for creativity.

THE NEW MIDDLE CLASS

More than 2 billion people in the emerging economies (more than 25 percent of the world population) will have entered the new middle class by 2030. It was estimated that in 2012, 60 million people entered the middle class in China alone. The new middle class is not just surviving economically; it has money left for healthcare, travel, shopping, learning, and insurance. And soon, these people will have a small car and their own house. Those in the new middle class are about to fulfill a material dream; they work hard, and they are prepared to wait for material rewards. They live by the extended now, in

contrast to the middle class in the West. Economically, they are moving gradually from survival to thriving. The American middle class is different; its members are wealthier, and they often define their status based on tradition and social position. Importantly, the new middle class in the emerging economies has a different pattern of consumption—and it includes products from the West. A huge mass market is emerging.

A WHOLE NEW WORLD IN MARKETING

Marketing and advertising is often described as a conservative business—people's needs and dreams remain much the same; only products change from time to time. Well, some changes do take place; events and social media are new tools. However, if we look forward 10 years and use extended now thinking, we will see that marketing and advertising will be transformed in two ways. The first is one-to-one communication. Amazon is doing this already. It notices what you are buying, and it sends you e-mails suggesting other products on the same subject. Since you are interested in this subject, we have another offer—if you will allow us to show it to you. When we allow Internet sites to take note of our interests, we get offers that are relevant and useful to us. There will be no more mass marketing. The second one is "fan clubs," communities and social sites that offer products or services, but that add value and a social network. Apple and Procter & Gamble are doing this already, as are a lot of sports clubs. In 10 years' time, we may have 10,000 or even 100,000 communities around the world, each with its own "personality"—act now. At best, you can change a customer into an ambassador, and at the same time

the company gets precious day-to-day information about consumer trends.

MEASURE HAPPINESS, NOT GDP

For the past 50 years, nations and governments have used GDP (material progress) as the yardstick for success. Politicians are somehow creating the illusion that they are the ones that are responsible for our economic growth. When a crisis comes, they blame somebody else. The fact is that GDP growth is created by people who are working hard (by you and me); governments play a minor role (if any), at least in Western democracies. In the rich part of the world, making more money does not make you happier and more satisfied with your life. Until you have enough, more money is important, but after that, happiness comes from other sources: relationships, family and friends, and a job with good colleagues.

In a postmodern world, it is logical to change the yardstick from GDP to happiness or satisfaction with life. We do have the figures for happiness and thriving, and politicians will just have to use them—they exist, and they are available. Gallup and World Values Survey are the major contributors. Why do we want more money? In order to live a happier life. When this is the case, then use a happiness index. China's growth rate is four times higher than that in the United States; however, Americans are happier. This is the political reason for the idea. It may take some time before the most admired country in the world becomes the one with the happiest citizens, but it will happen. Politicians of the future will promise to raise the happiness index if they are elected—a different political platform indeed.

RE-CREATE NATURE

The world population is moving from the countryside to the cities. Today, 50 percent of people are living in cities, and the United Nations expects this figure to be 70 percent as early as 2025. Construction and infrastructure are badly needed, but let us not forget about the countryside. In the rich part of the world, we want to visit nature; we admire it, and we study it. Unfortunately, a great deal of nature has been destroyed in the past 100 years—precious habitats for plants and animals. We want to re-create real nature, nature as it was before. We want to have forests, meadows, and lakes to visit when we leave the city for recreation. Nostalgia? Well, maybe, but it is an emerging market.

The Material World

Here is the global overview: in a globalized economy, the geography of wealth and poverty is the reason for trade, and it underlies the strategies of many U.S. companies. What consumers buy is determined by their income, and income is not distributed equally—far from it.

Chapter 1 presents a snapshot of the distribution of wealth among nations today and a long-term forecast: how rich will nations and their citizens be in 20 to 30 years, in the 2040s? We study the material, physical world: stuff, products, and services.

HOW RICH ARE WE NOW?

Imagine traveling between the extremes. You start in Bamako, the capital of Mali, a small nation in Western Africa and one of the poorest countries in the world. You fly to New York, one of the richest cities in the world. These are extremes; the

average New Yorker is more than 50 times wealthier than the average person in Bamako. The New Yorker need not worry about where his next meal is coming from; the person living in Bamako has to worry every day about getting enough to eat. This chapter presents an overview of the world economy: which nations are rich and poor just now and especially where the nations will be in the future—an inspiring look into the next 20 to 30 years. The world is the marketplace for many companies, and they will need to know the pattern of consumption. For any company that is taking an interest in the "extended now," this chapter will inspire its strategy. For all of us, a snapshot of the economy in a globalized world is a must if we want to understand the world and put our lives in perspective.

No company is isolated from the national and the world economy. If it is growing, so can your company. Of course it is possible to prosper during a recession, but this is the exception, not the rule. GDP is the best measure of our ability to buy things. What is the state of the world economy at the moment, and what are the prospects for the future? We do have a globally accepted system for measuring material values, both on the national level and internationally. Some experts criticize the way it is done, but the figures from the World Bank are the ones that economists and governments use. Can we forecast as much as 30 years ahead? The answer is, this is not an exact science, but long-term forecasts often have a better chance because we have a pattern from the past to help us. If you want to guess what the temperature will be next Tuesday, you may well fail, but if you are asked what the average temperature for 2018 will be, you are likely to succeed. It will not deviate much from what we know about past temperatures. The same rule applies to long-term forecasts for GDP.

Mr. or Mrs. World Average

For the average person in the world (the average consumer), GDP per capita today is about $10,000. Countries with GDP that is close to this global average are Brazil, Belarus, Costa Rica, Iran, and Lebanon. How can we understand this figure? What does $10,000 mean in practical terms? It is measured in terms of purchasing power parity (PPP) by the World Bank. It reflects how much you can afford to buy, irrespective of fluctuating currencies; it is real. The per capita figures are simply GDP divided by the size of the population (and remember that children are persons, too). Most people live in families. The five countries mentioned have an average household size of four or a little more; thus, the family income is about $40,000. How much can this family afford to buy? It can buy enough food, including meat; it will live in a small apartment or even a house, it can visit the doctor now and then, it will own bicycles and a motorbike, and it can afford education for the children, but it has no car, no holidays abroad, and no insurance.

Mr. and Mrs. Rich

The richest consumers, on average, have a per capita GDP of around $50,000. Countries close to this top of the world today are Norway, Kuwait, Singapore, and the United States. The household size will be between two and three persons, and the family will have two cars, travel abroad, own a house, be fully insured, and have a pension to look forward to.

Mr. and Mrs. Poor

The poorest of the poor in the world have a per capita GDP of about $700. They live in countries like Togo, Mali, Malawi,

Niger, and Ethiopia. Having enough to eat every day is a constant challenge for them, and their home has just one or two rooms for a family of perhaps five persons and may not have running water or electricity.

This huge gap between rich and poor is real; it's not just some figures in the economists' books. A GDP of $700 will buy the basic needs for survival, but not much else. If you have $50,000 per person, your family may have a Jacuzzi in the bathroom and shopping is a leisure activity; it's about your lifestyle.

Remember that these are national averages. There are a few people in Mali who are richer than some people in, say, Norway, but for most companies, the average is the more important figure.

This is a snapshot of the present. Let's move to the important question: how rich will we become in the future? When we talk about the growth for next year, listen to the economists, but when we are talking about the next 10 or 30 years, listen to the past, to the pattern as it has developed over time.

HOW RICH WILL WE BE IN THE 2040s, BASED ON PAST GROWTH PATTERNS?

Let us start with 1820; this is a good year, since it was the start of the Industrial Revolution in the United Kingdom—the beginning of a period in which economic growth was a normal thing. From 1820 to 2000, the average annual growth of GDP was highest in the Americas (North and South), a staggering figure of more than 3 percent. In the rest of the world, it was slightly above 2 percent. That is a lot for such a long period. Your income doubles in a little less than 25 years if growth is 3 percent per year. If it is 2 percent annually, it takes 35 years

for your income to double. (*Income* includes both what you can buy and the value of the services available from society, such as schools, roads, hospitals, and law and order.) In the 180 years between 1820 and 2000 the average world citizen has become about 50 times richer. The lesson from the past is clear: despite two world wars, local wars and revolutions, bad government, famine, diseases, and recessions, the economy is growing in the long term. Compared to our forebears, we are filthy rich. We would gladly give them some of our money if we could. Inheritances go to the next generation (for good reasons), but imagine if we could do it backward!

Can we expect this pattern of continuous economic growth to go on and on far into some distant future? Yes. For more than 180 years, we have seen a consistent pattern of growth. That is a solid base for looking ahead. What about pollution? We have started to clean up, and wind and solar power are included in the GDP. What about too many people on the planet? The growth of the world population is declining, and even when the population was growing fastest, GDP per person was growing fast too.

Let us look at some likely regional and national long-term growth figures.

China in the 2040s

China has been growing at a rate of nearly 10 percent for many years. Let us assume that China's GDP will grow 7 percent each year from $6,000 today (we can't be sure, but that is a sensible, conservative figure). In a little more than 30 years, China's average GDP per person will equal that of the richest nations today, like the United States, $50,000. But of course, as China has more than one billion consumers, the market for most products

and services will be much the same as that in Europe and North America combined. If we are less conservative and expect 10 percent growth annually for 30 years, the figure is more than $100,000. This is an awesome figure. In this optimistic case, China will surpass the United States in per capita income and will of course become the world's largest economy by far. The world's finance ministers will want to visit Beijing very often.

South Korea in the 2040s

Not only China but all of Asia is growing fast. South Korea's per capita GDP is currently about $25,000. If its economy grows at 4 percent (again, a cautious estimate), Koreans will be as wealthy as Americans in 30 years, with $81,000. The East is catching up. The question is, will high growth continue when the material needs of the majority have been satisfied? (Remember what happened to Japan.)

The United States in the 2040s

The United States has been growing at 2 to 3.5 percent for many years—actually a bit faster than Western Europe. If the United States grows by 2.0 percent for the next 30 years, the average U.S. GDP per person will go from $47,000 to $85,000.

Germany, France, Italy, and the United Kingdom in the 2040s

The big economies of Western Europe (Germany, France, Italy, and the United Kingdom) are expected, for a lot of reasons, to grow more slowly than the United States, at say 1.5 percent. At that rate, GDP per capita will grow from $34,000 to

$54,000 in 30 years. People in China and the big countries of Western Europe will be slightly less well off than Americans, but Europe will be on the same level as China, and South Koreans will become richer than people in Western Europe if our assumptions come true.

The Poorest in the 2040s

What about the poorest countries in 30 years, those with $700 per capita today? If we assume that they will have a growth rate of 5 percent (which is optimistic, but not unrealistic), the figure will be only $3,000, much like the per capita figure for India today. Catching up from a low point takes a long time. But for today's poor families in Africa, the difference is vital— from not enough to eat, to enough.

* * *

This way of extrapolating the past into the future of the world economy is "surprise-free." There may be surprises; we cannot be sure. Perhaps some economies will stop growing fast, as Japan's did 20 years ago. Perhaps the European Union will reinvent itself and become a successful innovator, "the European Lion" (the reader may smile). The future of growth and GDP levels is a scenario (a scenario says: given this assumption, which we deem likely, this will happen, and then this will be the situation in 30 years time). We are using history as the best yardstick available. The time horizon is long because it gives a clearer perspective— a better idea of the economic world as it may look in the 2040s, when the last veterans from World War II have died, when the last drops of oil and gas (we assume) have been pumped up from mother earth, when today's schoolchildren have grown up

and are managing the companies, when the 2010s are looked upon as "the good old days" and historians are writing books that tell us, no, they were really not that good.

Also, extrapolations provide us with an idea of what to expect during the next 10 years, irrespective of recessions, elections, and interest rates. When you wish to know about the economy in the next quarter or the next year, consult the economists; they will do their best.

In the 2040s, our economic world will have been transformed a lot. First and foremost, the economic gap between East and West will have disappeared. The Americas, Europe, and East and Southeast Asia will be nearly equally rich. There will be no need to move production from Europe to China any more, since labor costs will be about the same. Perhaps Africa will become the future "factory of the world."

Humanity has been around for 100,000 years or a little longer. But for most of this time (actually about 99,800 years), there was no permanent material progress—that started just 200 years ago with the factories in England and Scotland. It is a fantastic story of material success, and we can expect it to continue for many years to come. Unfortunately, it is not the end of poverty in the world, but fewer people will be poor and the aid programs can focus on just a few areas.

THE BIG NATIONS IN THE GLOBAL ECONOMY

If we look at the size of national economies instead of at the personal level, the United States today is by far the largest economy—nearly two times bigger than the second largest, China, when measured in PPP terms. In 30 years' time, China will

surpass the United States, even assuming a growth rate of 5 percent for China and 2 percent for the United States. The result is that we will have two economic colossi, the United States and China, one the economic leader of the West and one of the East.

In times of crisis in the mature economies, even some experts are suggesting that stagnation or even recessions will continue—that the period of growth that began 200 years ago is about to end. Admittedly, this is a risk, but the more likely future is growth. Downturns have never lasted; even the Great Depression in the 1930s ended, and so will the recession that we are currently in. However, high growth rates for the West depend on something new happening—a new dream, a new nonmaterial dream.

Economic inequality among nations is narrowing. Recent figures say that per capita PPP is $1,500 in low-income countries with 1.3 billion people, $6,000 in middle-income countries with 4.3 billion people, and $36,000 in high-income countries with 1 billion people. Recent growth patterns indicate annual growth figures per capita of 4.2 percent for low-income countries, 7.2 percent for middle-income countries, and 1.8 percent for high-income countries. We can expect this narrowing to continue, but of course the gap between poor and rich will remain for the next 30 years. The gap between rich and poor nationally is tending to increase in many countries, including the United States, but the international trend is the opposite.

BOOM AND DOOM: THE ETERNAL CYCLE

Average growth means average, not the same every year. Let's look at the likely fluctuations. Imagine a walk on Wall Street. Here we find many bank headquarters and the famous New

York Stock Exchange with its impressive Roman columns. It looks like a temple—and it is. It is a building that signals trust, and it appears timeless. But is it timeless, and can we always trust the buildings with the Roman columns? The pillars of trust? Normally, we can trust them, but not always. When is not always? Average figures for growth are useful—they give us an idea of direction—but they are averages; sometimes the figures are a bit higher, and sometimes they are zero or even negative. When do downturns happen, and can we predict them?

During the 1970s, macroeconomists fell in love with physics. They wanted to transform their research into something as scientific as physics. For this they needed computers, mathematics, and models, complicated ones. These models did the forecasting for GDP and for the stock exchange. They got more and more sophisticated, and the idea developed that we now had the tools for precise forecasting. Macroeconomics had arrived; it was science—almost. When the models failed (and they still did), we would come up with an improved one.

OK, the models did help, but most economists forgot about the old ways. There is another tool that is equally important and illuminating: simple empirical research—the study of economic history and the business cycles of the past. History tells us a lot, especially that ups and downs have always existed. They follow each other as surely as winter follows autumn. During the ups, most economists tell us that "this time it is different": the government has much more precise figures and more resources, and the banks have got almost perfect forecasting instruments, so there will be no more recessions. Trust us. You shouldn't.

Economics is not an exact science; it is about human behavior as well. You need to get into the brains of bankers, regulators, and investors and determine how they think. We

haven't been there, but one human factor is obvious: greed. It is embedded in our DNA. We cannot remove it; it is a fact; it is part of our lives. Such a thing as "economic man" (the rational decision maker) does not exist in isolation. We go to the casino, we play lotto, we gamble, although we know very well that the likely outcome is loss. Still we do it and come back; memory is short. *Homo sapiens* is emotional and rational at the same time. That's how we are.

According to the U.S. National Bureau of Economic Research, a recession is defined as a fall in GDP for two or more consecutive quarters. Older contractions are just referred to as troughs. The figures say that the United States has had 47 contractions since 1790. That is one every 4.6 years. Of course, the foundations of the economy have changed a lot over the years, so let us look at some more recent figures. Between the beginning of the Great Depression (1929) and 2009, we have had 14 recessions; that is one every 5.7 years. Since 1945, we have had 11 recessions; that is one every 5.8 years. These recessions lasted on average 10.9 months.

The trend is toward longer periods of growth (an average of almost 6 years since 1945). One lesson is crystal clear, however: recessions are normal; they are part of the pattern. The averages tell us that the next recession will come in 2018, if we believe our history and not the experts telling us that "this time it is different." If we consider the extremes since 1945, the longest growth period was 10 years (during the 1990s) and the shortest was 1 year (1981–1982). Most figures are close to the average, though.

According to this history lesson, we are unable to learn anything. We repeat our mistakes; we stay too long at the casino even though every gambling expert in Las Vegas will tell you that the only way to beat the odds is to leave the table when you have won.

These are figures from the United States, but those for Europe and elsewhere are similar; the same pattern has been repeating itself continuously since 1790 and even earlier.

What can you do? Prepare for 2018. This is the clever lesson, and if everybody did it, it would not happen, but it will. This proves that, on average, we are human.

The "tulip mania" of 1636–1637 tells us all about the source of periodic recessions—why they happen. This one happened almost 400 years ago. In February 1637, a single tulip bulb could sell for as much as a skilled craftsman could earn in several years. Up until then, everybody believed that the price of these precious tulip bulbs would go up forever—it was safe to buy them at almost any price. After February 1637, the market lost its faith in the value of tulip bulbs; there were no buyers anymore, and the bubble burst suddenly. This is an iconic illustration of a speculative economic bubble. Pete Seeger could have written his song "Where Have All the Flowers Gone?" and its concluding line, "When will we ever learn?" in 1637. Another illustrative story: in 2009, market capitalization on U.S. stock markets was a staggering $15 trillion and stocks changed hands every four months during that year. People didn't have much patience, but legal gambling isn't limited to Las Vegas.

THE MULTIPOLAR WORLD OF ECONOMIC GROWTH—THE MEANING OF GLOBALIZATION

The estimated growth figures indicate that we are moving toward a multipolar world in economic terms. It also tells us that trade between East and West will be much greater than

it is now and that we may see a new collaboration between businesses and governments. We often hear that the United States is the innovator of the world, China is the producer, and India provides the services. In addition, we have the energy exporters in the Middle East and Russia. This may be partly true today, but the real perspective for the future is this: 500 years ago, China and other parts of East and Southeast Asia and India were just as rich as Europe. There was a balance of wealth, although with limited East-West trade. Expect this balance to be restored in 30 years, this time with the East taking part in the global trade. At the moment, global exports (and thus imports) are about 20 percent of world GDP. When GDP growth is 4 percent, trade grows twice as much or more, on average. This is globalization; it is an ongoing process. If the world economy has at least doubled by 2040, trade will be four times what it is now, and this means increased economic and political interdependence. This is how it looks now; the figures may be a little higher or a little lower, but this is the surprise-free projection.

A surprise might happen if major countries changed their political system away from free markets and an open economy. Overall, tariffs are currently only around 3 percent globally, but of course there are many other obstacles to free trade. Political conflicts, natural disasters, epidemics, and even wars do not affect the projection much, however. This is what the history of economic growth tells us.

How will this affect business during the next 10 years? The demand for industrial products in the East is growing; this is where people need cars, trains, airplanes, better homes, and household appliances. Expect global companies in these industries to be headquartered here. This is where the largest and fastest-growing markets will be located. Will General Motors

and Microsoft move to Shanghai? Possibly, but in the long term (30 years), they may move back.

The market for services (like shipping, IT services, information, education, banking, entertainment, research, tourism, cleaning, accounting, and insurance) is different. At the moment, it is less open to international trade, and some services, such as tourism, are not easy to export.

It is a trade world, an economic world with competition among the 500 largest corporations, assisted by governments, more or less. Politics is driven by economic interest, not the other way round.

The source of forecasts for the next few years is the World Bank. Its conclusion is that the world economy is expected to be back on track by 2012 or 2013. That means world growth of 3.5 to 4.0 percent and trade growth of around 10 percent. The West is expected to grow by 1 to 3 percent and India and China by 8 to 10 percent in 2012.

We are facing huge structural changes during the next years. The world's urban population is expected to grow 5 percent to 5.5 percent in 10 years. At least 500 million more people will live in cities.

Another way of explaining the structural changes in the world economy is where the jobs are. Agriculture amounts to 25 percent of GDP in low-income countries, 9 percent in middle-income countries, and 1 percent in high-income countries. In 10 years, the figure for low-income countries may fall to 10 percent and that for middle-income countries to 5 percent.

Manufacturing is 16 percent of GDP in low-income countries, 19 percent in middle-income countries, and 17 percent in high-income countries. Expect it to fall about 2 percentage points or more in 10 years.

The largest share of the world economy is the contribution from services: 75 percent. It will increase during the next 10 years and in the long term will dominate the world economy. This is a gradual process. Let us combine these four trends:

◆ Global companies grow bigger (concentration of ownership) and thus become more influential.
◆ The link between governments and companies is strong, especially outside the Western Hemisphere. A lot of fast-growing companies are owned by governments.
◆ International trade is growing twice as fast as global GDP.
◆ Access to resources like oil, water, grain, and some metals is seen as more important.

The result is perhaps not a parallel United Nations for big companies called "United Corporations" (although this is certainly a possibility), but business influencing national and international decision making a lot more than it does today. It is the era of lobbyists and commercial diplomacy.

GROWTH HAPPENS IN CITIES

The move away from agriculture tells us where we want to live. *Homo sapiens* is not an endangered species—there are nearly 2 billion more of us than there were 10 years ago. There are a little more than 7 billion of us on this earth, and the consensus is that the number will continue to grow until there are 9 to 10 billion in 50 years' time. Where will all these people live? The answer is clear: in cities. A few years ago, a certain unknown individual moved away from the countryside, and

the statisticians said, "Now more than 50 percent are living in cities." UN experts are predicting that in 2025, 70 percent of the world's population will live in cities.

A hundred years ago, the trek to the cities took place in Europe and North America. Poor farmers knew that the opportunity to have a better life was in the towns, with their factories. Now the same thing is happening in the emerging economies in Asia. The urban growth rate in the West is 1 percent per year or less, while that in the East is 2.5 to 3.5 percent. In East Asia, the urban population is growing by 50 million each year. That is the size of the population of South Korea or Ukraine.

There is a lot of talk about "mega-cities," but only 20 percent of the world's population lives in cities with more than 1 million people; the rest lives in smaller places. The largest cities today have around 20 million inhabitants, including suburbs. We may expect urban megaregions in the future when one city merges with its neighbor. One example is São Paulo and Rio de Janeiro in Brazil; an urbanized corridor between the two may emerge. The same is happening in Japan with Nagoya, Osaka, Kyoto, and Kobe.

Why the city? The answer is obvious: machines are taking over jobs in farming, and the new jobs are being created in or near the city. People move there in order to work and have an income. In most cities, GDP per person is much higher than it is in rural areas; people are moving to where the money is, and a great deal of higher education takes place in cities.

When people move to the city, they experience new things, new lifestyles, and new ways of doing business; a city is a stimulating place, and it is a place for innovation and creativity. The rural areas are the opposite: static; they are about tradition and routine—doing the same thing better, improving but not innovating. The city environment is dynamic.

The slums in many cities are a problem, but most people move to the city because the possibilities in farming are even worse. Dealing with slums is a political and humanitarian challenge, but progress is possible because most slums are in high-growth economies. It may get worse in some cities before it gets better, though.

Most big cities with high-rise buildings have problems with traffic congestion even when they have good public transportation. What is needed is fewer high-rise buildings and more space, more centers, larger urban areas, and more suburbs. City planners should think horizontal instead of vertical. The ideal may be the "garden city"—it may be large, but it has more breathing space than we find in today's megacities. Actually, the headquarters of a lot of big businesses are not in the town center. Think of Silicon *Valley* or Microsoft—they are located in suburbs.

The city is not about the "creative class"—no class or group has a monopoly on creativity; we can all be creative. It is about creating innovative environments. Cinemas, theaters, and cafés are extras, not a precondition for innovation. The small city of Oulu in Northern Finland is a fantastic place for innovation. It attracts creative people and companies from around the world, but with its cold and dark winters, it is not exactly a playground.

TEXTILES, CARS, AND ELECTRONICS— INDUSTRIES ON THE MOVE

Reports from the United Nations conclude that Ukraine is one of the most important breadbaskets of the world because of its fertile soil, the so-called black earth. If we look at grain

production in Ukraine, it is currently about 40 million tons per year, but the potential is estimated to be more than double that—around 100 million tons. That is a lot; it will feed 400 million people and provide nearly all of what the citizens of the European Union need. Will agriculture move east and EU grain production decline dramatically? It is possible, since Ukraine is the more efficient place to produce grain. It needs investment and access to the European market, but at some point it will happen—when markets for agricultural products open up. It may take some time, though. Production of manufactured products is moving geographically faster than agriculture is because there are fewer trade barriers. Let us have a look at not only the future of the world's breadbaskets but also the future of the world's factories. Where will they be located in, say, 10 years' time?

Let us consider just a few industries. The textile industry started in the 1760s with the multispool spinning wheel—the "spinning jenny." It was a crucial part of England's Industrial Revolution. Later the "rag trade" moved to Europe and the United States. Now it has moved to Asia and especially China, and the textile factories in the West are disappearing—not all of them, but most. The reasons are, as always, productivity. Wages are lower in Asia at the moment, but with GDP growing by 8 to 10 percent each year in China and India (10 percent makes for a doubling of income every seven years), the long-term future of the Asian textile industry is 10 to 15 years. Who will take over? The obvious guess is Africa, in particular Southern Africa. Other possibilities are Central Asia and North Africa.

The world market for new cars (passenger and commercial vehicles) is more than 70 million per year. The world is on

wheels—more so than on rails. If the life expectancy of a car is 15 years, we will soon all be able to sit in a car (not in comfort, though). Large-scale production started in the United States with Henry Ford and spread to Europe. Today the largest car market is China, and it will remain so for many years to come (in China, only 24 persons in a thousand own a car). Since car production is large-scale on long assembly lines, we can expect China to remain the world's number one car manufacturer. Production could decline in the United States and in Europe as a consequence. A more automated assembly line with fewer employees could delay the shift, but the factories must be located near this fast-growing market. At the moment, container traffic (measured by the number of standardized 20-foot containers) at Chinese ports is more than 100 million per year; in the United States, it is less than half of that figure. The balance of world trade is shifting.

If we look at high-tech exports (defined as aerospace, computers, pharmaceutical products, instruments, and electrical equipment), China is again the world leader. This definition counts a lot of consumer electronics as high-tech; some really are, but it also includes a lot of products that are not usually seen as high-tech anymore. Still, the booming market for computers (2 billion computers are expected worldwide by 2015, nearly a doubling) will increasingly be served from China, Japan, South Korea, Singapore, Malaysia, India, and other East Asian countries.

If nothing unexpected happens, China's GDP will overtake that of the United States in less than 10 years. The average American will still be wealthier than the average Chinese citizen, however. Which country will become the master of the world—if either? The power centers have always been rotating

slowly but surely, like a glacier. In the West, it was Egypt for more than a thousand years, and then the baton was passed to the Roman Empire; later it was in the hands of the city-states of Northern Italy and the Netherlands. Because of the successful Industrial Revolution, the center of power moved to the United Kingdom 200 years ago. In the last century it moved to the United States, and this great country is the center today and will remain so for perhaps the next 20 to 30 years. In the East, China lost momentum 500 years ago and is right now catching up fast. The economy has become global, and we can expect a gradual (very gradual) shift from the United States to China and other Asian countries. It has been said before, but it is true: this century belongs to the United States *and* China.

New ideas always come dressed in rags. They don't look like much in the beginning. Traditionally, we often speak of the spiritual East, the birthplace of Hinduism and Buddhism, in contrast to the materialistic West. This may be reversed in the foreseeable future: the new spiritual West and the materialistic East. The West and soon also the East will move away from GDP and wealth as a measure of success. This is not the end of consumption, or even of consumerism. We will still need products and services (don't worry), but not the ones we see today. It will be stuff that enhances our well-being, our quality of life. What makes people happy? Basically, a belief in themselves and their own values. In the ancient temple of Apollo in Delphi, Greece, the words "know thyself" were written on the entrance. It was true then, and it is true now. This is the source of true well-being. Imagine the current race to dominate the world economy being transformed into a race for well-being. The region or country with the highest personal well-being will be the winner—the most human society of them all.

THE NEW GLOBAL MIDDLE CLASS—THE 2 BILLION PEOPLE MARKET OPPORTUNITY

Looking at the growth pattern presented in this chapter, we may ask if there is a group of consumers that is emerging from poverty—a group that is not exactly getting rich, but that has money left after basic needs have been satisfied. The obvious answer is the new middle class in the emerging economies. A middle-class revolution is happening right now in the emerging economies. It is about millions of families suddenly discovering that the gate to a new and better life is wide open. A life with much higher standard of living is becoming a reality. This is taking place in all countries with fast-growing market economies. Politically, it opens the door to stability, low inflation, tolerance, and corruption-free institutions, but not necessarily democracy. In brief, the future will bring a decent life in which people can enjoy the fruits of hard work.

Who is the middle class in emerging economies? People with incomes of between $6,000 and $30,000 in PPP terms; that means that they have money to spend after buying the things that are essential for life. An astonishing 2 billion people could join this middle class by 2030; that is more than 25 percent of the world's population. Let's look more closely at these exciting figures.

In 2011, more than 150 million people globally will cross the $3,000 threshold, more than 100 million will cross the $6,000 barrier, and 80 million will make more than $9,000. Most of them live in China and India. In China, new entrants to the middle class (more than $3,000) are peaking right now, with 60 million people per year. India's peak is expected a little later, in 2030, but the figure for 2020 could be as high as

40 million. The figures for other emerging economies are much lower: from 2 to 4 million per country. The reason is that many of these countries have fewer poor people to cross the threshold. They include South Korea, Brazil, Iran, Mexico, Turkey, and Vietnam. The countries to watch are China and India.

Today the middle class is mostly urban, but gradually these people will move to the suburbs, commute to work, own their houses, visit malls, and save money for education, health services, and tourism. They will buy consumer electronics, a small car, and insurance, and they will have a credit card or two.

The other middle class—the Western one—is different. The household income of the people in this group today is between $17,000 and $70,000 (in PPP terms), but they often define their status as "middle class" by profession or tradition, not income. Even if the middle class in the emerging economies aspires to Western-style products and brands—and it certainly will—the products will have to be different for economic and cultural reasons. Within nations, income inequality may increase, but globally, the opposite is happening. The world is becoming much more equal than it used to be.

The rich Western middle class is entering the postmaterialistic era. The emerging economies' middle class is entering the materialistic one. This is one of the truly positive developments in this decade. These people are the "stable class"; they don't look to government for money and employment; they work hard in the fast-growing private sector for themselves and their family; they are the new consumers. Just now they are taking a giant step upward in Maslow's famous hierarchy of needs. From basic needs and the need for safety, they are moving to the next step: the need for self-esteem, self-confidence, achievement, and respect for values other than their own. In short, they are moving from survival to a positive, forward-looking,

open state of mind—to hope, to setting goals for the future, and to economic freedom.

The Western middle class rose in the last century; now the same thing is happening in most of the rest of the world, but on a much grander scale. Imagine a world with 1.5 billion rich people, 5 billion representing the new middle class, and less than 1 billion poor. We are not there yet, but soon we may see this middle class dominate the world economy and politics. How will these people live their lives, and how will they spend their money?

Those in this new middle class will go shopping. The family-owned corner store will turn into a mall owned by a big company. Will the owners be the Walmarts, the Carrefours, the Metro AGs, or the Tescos of the Western world, or will they be Asian corporations? If a retail chain is global (a Chinese firm with stores in Europe and the United States or vice versa), how is centralized decision making possible? It is not. Some of the brands will be the same, but most products and services will have to be different. The truly decentralized global retail company has yet to be invented. Is it possible to create a company without a global headquarters? The retail industry will show us the limits of globalization.

The people in this new middle class want their children to go to college. Currently, 400,000 young Chinese are studying abroad, and soon we will see more East-West collaboration in the majority of institutions of higher education. Asian institutions of learning in the West and Western ones in Asia will transform traditional academic life forever. Perhaps education will become the largest industry at some time in the not too far distant future. For elementary schools, we are already seeing a clash between Eastern and Western systems and principles. When a school can be exported like a product, the result will

be fierce competition, both locally and at the national level. Don't expect it to happen tomorrow for political and language reasons, but it will happen.

The new middle class wants to see the world. The biggest market for cars is already China, and soon India will join it. The $3,000 car will soon become the $4,000 car, and in 15 to 20 years, the largest car producer by far will be in China or in India. Asia will be on wheels. In 2011, one billion people traveled internationally. In round figures, half of them were from advanced economies and half from emerging ones. In 10 years, the vast majority of travelers will come from the emerging economies. This is not enough to ensure global harmony and understanding, but it is a welcome contribution.

These people want access to good healthcare, and they will pay for it. The cost of healthcare in most countries is between 6 and 12 percent of GDP. It is a huge industry that includes primary care, the pharmaceutical industry, pharmacies, doctors, and hospitals. The new middle class is entering healthcare in a big way. In 10 to 20 years' time, we may see a few big hospital chains with perhaps 10,000 hospitals around the world. As in the car industry, size matters in purchasing, research, and standardization.

The new global middle class wants to protect its wealth. Insurance will become affordable and a must; you will need a bank loan and a credit card to finance your consumption and your investments. You will ask for financial services.

And the new middle class will move to the suburbs—people will want a house for their family.

CYBERSECURITY

Modern nations are dependent on roads, railways, and infrastructure, but, equally important, they are also dependent on

lines of communication. We must trust the lines of communication; they must be secure. Physical security and what is called cybersecurity are both necessities, and the distinction is becoming blurred.

Think about your daily life. Suppose you woke up one morning and found all your connections down. You would have no access to your smartphone and no access to phone numbers, addresses, your calendar, and e-mail—not to mention more personal things, such as photos, bank accounts, and text messages. Would you panic? Many of us would.

For us to be able to transmit data, control over the generation and flow of electricity is required. We also need computer hardware, communication links, and software to process data. Where do you draw the line between physical security and cybersecurity? And does such a line make sense anymore?

Physical security traditionally means protecting assets from physical damage. Cybersecurity typically means protecting both physical and cyber assets from operational failure or manipulation caused by unauthorized access to software or data. A response to a physical threat to security would be installing a fence; a response to a cyberthreat would be installing firewall software.

At the moment, several countries are considering asserting control over the communications of citizens and corporations on the Internet. In the United Kingdom, there has been a debate about how cyberattacks by individuals or rogue states could affect healthcare, transportation, or defense systems. Similarly, in the United States, legislators have been debating what rights should be given to the U.S. president to deal with attacks on the Internet.

Our critical information infrastructure systems will be more vulnerable in the future for two reasons. First, more content from multiple and varied sources will be housed together on

the customer and end-user side, creating a highly complex security environment. As information and communications technology and CII systems grow ever more interconnected and embedded in vital services from finance to energy, the level of systemic risk and the potential for a cascade of failures are increasing. Second, the complexity of supply chains has led to a situation in which intellectual property developers, software platform vendors, application vendors, and network operators are all trying to offload on each other, while the end users have little information about or power over the risk they are exposing themselves to. If nothing is done, this asymmetry may develop intolerably. Perhaps WikiLeaks is just the beginning.

Since WikiLeaks.org went online, it has published a huge number of documents. Nearly all of them are, if not secret, at least sensitive to those involved. The range of documents varies from standard operating procedures at Guantánamo Bay to the "Climategate" e-mails at the University of East Anglia and even the contents of Sarah Palin's e-mails.

The French minister Eric Besson considers WikiLeaks's work dangerous and unethical and has taken actions to disable its operations. However, so far, legal attempts to stop it have not been successful. WikiLeaks has not complied with legal requests from the Church of Scientology, any more than it has complied with similar demands from Swiss banks, Russian offshore stem-cell centers, or the Pentagon.

In Kenya, a politician vowed to sue after Assange published a confidential report alleging that President Daniel arap Moi had moved billions of dollars out of the country into his own bank account.

However, the site's work in Kenya earned it an award from Amnesty International.

The Values of Nations: "How Are We?"

Chapter 1 presented an overview of wealth and poverty—of global, national, and per person GDP. That is the material world. This chapter looks at the nonmaterial world, our values: what we believe in, what we like, and what we don't like. It is about emotions, about happiness, equality, and trust. We study cultural differences and the important changes that are likely to take place. Our values, together with our income, what we consume, and what we buy, define us. Let's begin with the big picture!

A SPRINT THROUGH HISTORY AND INTO THE FUTURE OF GLOBAL VALUES

Let us make this as brief as possible with a narrative in three scenes. You may define your life by the things you own or the

money you make—the more the better. That is emphasizing materialist values, the materialist person. Or you may define your life by your level of happiness and your satisfaction with life. That is emphasizing nonmaterialist or postmaterialist values, the nonmaterialist person.

Scene 1: The Nonmaterialist Plateau

Just a few hundred years ago, before the Industrial Revolution, life was static for the vast majority of the people in the world. Material progress was not possible; most people were farmers, tilling the fields and tending the livestock. Kings, wars, and especially nature decided their living conditions; sometimes the harvest was good, and sometimes it was bad. There were ups and downs, but there was no expectation that the next generation would be better off. Historians can confirm that, yes, some progress happened, but it would not be experienced during one lifetime. As the English philosopher Thomas Hobbes said, life was "nasty, brutish and short." By today's standards, 99 percent of the world's population was poor according to the criteria defined by the United Nations.

Religion and spiritual things, however, were flowering; religion, faith, spirits, witches, and omens were with people and in their thoughts every day. Nature was a part of this spirituality; there were spirits in the forests and on the moors. People's hopes and fears and their fate were decided (more or less, but mostly more) by religion and faith. This is not surprising, since their material conditions could not be improved on a permanent basis. There was no need to emphasize the material aspect of life. In short, the average person was poor, yet nonmaterialistic. This is not to say that people were happy; death came early and unexpectedly, serious illnesses were common,

and there was little freedom. However, it was a life with a lot of thinking about spiritual matters, whether strictly religious or not.

Scene 2: Descent into the Valley of Materialism

With the Industrial Revolution, something completely new happened. It became possible to earn more and more money and to buy things that made life easier and more pleasant. This did not happen overnight, but it happened gradually, starting in the United Kingdom and spreading to the rest of the world, or at least most of it. It was possible to become rich, or at least to live better that your parents and forefathers.

The idea of economic growth was born, and the race to acquire things for your family began. This could happen not because you were part of the nobility or because of fate, but because you were smart and worked hard. For millennia people had worried about having enough to eat the next day or the next winter. Now there was a promise of enough, even plenty.

We rushed into the valley of materialism, the valley of material progress, acquiring cars, airplanes, television, telephones, sewers, central heating, computers, and travel. The Industrial Revolution led to other revolutions that created numerous technological innovations, including the electronic and digital revolutions. Life was about economic progress, and when this is important, even vital, we need to measure it. In the last century, GDP as a measure of material welfare came to be used as the yardstick for success for nations, persons, and companies. A bumper sticker on a car in California said it: "He who dies with the most toys wins." However, something new is happening—a new era is dawning. Materialism rules—but its rule is about to end.

Scene 3: The New Nonmaterialistic Plateau

A small part of the world's population is leaving the valley of materialism, and soon many others will follow. Some time this century, most of us will have left the valley of materialism and reached a new plateau where the old materialistic ways are looked down upon, where thinking about stuff will be called old-fashioned, so last century. It will not happen tomorrow, but it has begun, and it is most likely to be the megatrend for our century.

It is not a new hippie movement; we will still need a lot of things, but we will take them for granted and look for more important matters in our lives. Is a bigger car a goal in life? Is a big beef better than a small one? Should we care for nature and the environment? Is money the reason for working? All these questions are being asked, first by only a few, but gradually this will turn into a movement and our way of defining the good life will have changed forever. We will have reached the new nonmaterialistic plateau. Luckily, it is not like the first plateau because this time our material wealth will make life pleasant, more or less, but we will be asking the next question: when material things can be taken for granted, what dreams should determine our lives? A new spirituality, emotions, ideas, art, beauty, care, recognition, love, and imagination are part of the answer. People are both body and spirit. The spiritual aspect of humanity is coming back to us.

GDP is the traditional materialistic yardstick, but when it is seen as less important, we need new means of measuring progress. What is now vital for our lives? As we would expect, these new yardsticks are already available for us to study. Politicians are beginning to give them a little attention, and in a not too far distant future they will use them as the primary tool for

policy making. These global figures will be refined, but they are already an important answer to the eternal puzzle: how are we fulfilling our dreams today, and how will we be fulfilling them in the next 10 years?

HAPPINESS AND SATISFACTION WITH LIFE

A few international organizations measure happiness, satisfaction with life, or whether you are thriving, struggling, or suffering. They do this simply by asking people what they feel. They do so continuously. There are surveys by two respected organizations, Gallup, with its global wellbeing survey, and the World Values Survey Association, and they report on a nearly global scale; they have data on most nations. What can they tell us?

+ The degree of happiness or satisfaction with life does not change a lot over time. There is no close relationship between rising GDP and increasing happiness. But on the other hand, poor countries are generally less happy than rich ones.

+ At a certain level of GDP per person, more money does not mean much more happiness, but most nations have not reached this level yet. The level is about $15,000 to $20,000 per person. Above this level, human relations count a lot: family, friends, and trust in other people.

If we assume that "the pursuit of happiness," not becoming a millionaire, is our goal in life, then which countries are the happiest—the richest in happiness and thriving?

Those Very Rich in Thriving

According to the Gallup global well-being survey, in 2010, the top five countries were Denmark (72 percent), Sweden (69 percent), Canada (69 percent), Australia (65 percent), and Finland (64 percent). The figures show the percentage of the adult population responding that they are thriving, not struggling or suffering. Three of these (and probably four, since Norway is not included in the survey) are Nordic countries. In these countries, the weather is cold and taxes are high, which makes for a high degree of economic equality; furthermore, they are small countries. Vacations are long, education is mostly free, and the social welfare system takes care of the less fortunate. The most striking finding is perhaps their high levels of individualism and trust. In the Nordic countries, parents educate their children to follow their own path, and they trust their neighbors and friends. You can develop your own skills and values and still get respect from others. Individualism is allowed. Can these values be marketed and exported? Can they become a "product" in a postmaterialist world? Yes, but innovative ideas are required.

Those Less Rich in Thriving

In the range between 50 and 60 percent thriving, we find a mixed group. Yes, the United States and the United Kingdom are in this intermediate group, but so are Brazil, Venezuela, Mexico, and the Netherlands. Even though the three Latin American countries are significantly poorer than the United States, people there thrive just as much. Why are nations with a fourth of the GDP per person just as happy as the wealthy United States? One explanation is that money wealth is

relative—you compare yourself only with your neighbor, not with very rich people.

Those Poor in Thriving

These are mainly the money-poor nations of Africa, Asia, and Eastern Europe. When you are hungry and you lack access to clean water and medical facilities, it is impossible for you to answer that you are satisfied with your life. In Africa, most countries are in the range of 1 to 9 percent; in the Americas, in Asia, and in Eastern Europe, there are just a few in this range.

The range from rich to poor in happiness is huge, just as it is when we count money (count GDP). It would be fine if we could just say that along with economic growth come satisfaction with life and happiness. That is true for the poor part of the world, but the statistics do not support this theory in the money-rich countries. The richest countries are not the happiest. If they were, the United States should be much higher on the list, the Nordic countries somewhat lower, and some Latin American countries much lower. As more and more people become postmaterialist, we will have to look into this problem. We need the answers, the toolbox for achieving human happiness not just for the few, because more and more people, especially in the emerging economies, are reaching the GDP level where more money does not make them happier.

Which Are the Equality-Rich Countries?

The most equality-rich countries are the Nordic countries; they have few rich and few poor people, based on the respected Gini coefficient published by the World Bank. This indicates that when high taxes make it difficult to become a millionaire,

people become happier. There is less possibility that you will envy your neighbor. This would be an important political message if we could be sure that it was a key to happiness, and it may be. It is too early to draw this conclusion, but it is probably part, although not all, of the answer.

Which Are the Trust-Rich Countries?

Any society will do better and thrive if people can trust one another, exchange products without too much paperwork, and talk freely to their friends and neighbors. If you trust other people, life becomes easier and happier. When you ask, "Can most people be trusted?" (as the World Values Survey does), the Nordic countries are again on top, but so are China, Vietnam, Switzerland, and New Zealand. The winner is Norway: 74 percent say that "most people can be trusted."

The next group is some European countries and the United States, Canada, Australia, Indonesia, Thailand, and Japan. The U.S. figure is 39 percent, significantly lower than the figures from the top group. The countries with little trust are some African and Latin American countries.

The Postmaterialist Countries and the Materialist Ones

When you ask, "Is the first thing you are looking for in a job a 'good income'?" and the answer is yes, it indicates a materialist approach to life. The materialist winners are Ukraine (65 percent), Russia (57 percent), and some poor countries. Among the postmaterialist countries (those where people are looking for something other than a "good income"), the winners are again the Nordic countries, but also Brazil, France, Japan, Peru, Switzerland, and Taiwan.

THE NOT-FOR-PROFIT
COMPANY OF THE FUTURE

When more and more people leave the valley of materialism, companies will still need some profit in order to exist, but they will do it with an idea—a nonmaterial one. It could be superior craftsmanship, animal welfare, or helping the local community or the world's poor. It could be that the company's purpose is to empower people, to allow them to thrive in their lives. The company will still have a product or a service to sell, but that will really be a by-product. The real product will be the idea and the values it represents; that will be why people buy it, why employees love to work for the company, and why investors invest in it.

This movement has begun. Take just one example: Wikipedia, the online encyclopedia with tens of thousands of contributors. Why are these people doing this? Why not make it into a for-profit company? The "employees" (the volunteers) do it for reasons other than money. After millennia of striving for material things, this is a fantastic change of logic. When the respected U.S. business magazine *Fortune* chooses to change its title to *Thriving*, it will have happened, but this may take some time.

For the next 10 years, the vast majority of the companies in this world will remain for-profit companies, especially in the emerging economies. Gradually, however, companies in the West will choose to appeal to the new nonmaterial consumers and employees. This has already started softly, with ads telling consumers that the company supports this or that charity or that it respects nature and the environment, but gradually this will increase and the nonmaterial raison d'être will dominate marketing and corporate culture. It will be a gradual thing, since the transformation will be of a magnitude never experienced before.

THE FLAT SOCIETY—WHEN
HIERARCHIES FLATTEN

Since the Middle Ages, through the Enlightenment, and since the Industrial Revolution, one slow-moving trend can be observed: there is less respect for authority. This means people's respect for kings and the church, for bosses, teachers, police, politicians, and parents. More and more people have come to decide for themselves. This trend is confirmed by modern analysis. New means of communication, including the social media, have accelerated this trend toward the flat society. It is an important part of the pattern of values. All cultures are becoming flatter, but the levels (the starting point) are highly different.

At the national and international level, we can observe three all-important trends:

+ Democratic governments are less hierarchical than dictatorships, by definition. According to Freedom House, an American nongovernmental organization (NGO), the number of "free countries" has increased from 29 percent of countries evaluated in 1972 to 45 percent in 2010. It's a long-term trend, slow but solid.
+ The number of internationally operating NGOs is estimated to be 40,000. The national ones number in the millions, and both types are growing fast. The national governments and the international organizations are not alone. Call it citizen power.
+ Government spending as a share of GDP has grown fast in most mature economies, from 28 percent in 1960 to nearly 50 percent in 2010. The figures for the United States and Sweden are 42 percent and 53 percent,

respectively. The first reaction against big government has been "privatization," but the next trend will be much more innovative. It will be the self-organizing community, where citizens come together and form a volunteer service without the need for approval from government. This community could provide schools, care, security, arts, environmental protection, or tourism. The flat society has begun.

NEW TECHNOLOGY AS THE EQUALIZER: THE FLAT MARKETPLACE

Barriers of entry to the marketplace are being lowered by the Internet and social media. The price of developing a home page and setting up an online shop is coming down every month. Most companies are already using social media, and in a few years more than a billion of the world's people will be doing so. In the old days, for music, film, and books, you needed a publisher to approve your work and give you access to the marketplace. You don't need them anymore. Anybody with talent can reach the marketplace—and it does not cost a lot. More and more music bands are promoting themselves via social media. You can publish your book online—we can all become authors and directors. You can start an online news service. There's no need for a big publishing house. Fashion can be created in the social media and may be adopted later by the traditional fashion houses. Innovation starts from below.

The company gets reliable, innovative, and up-to-date market intelligence from the social media. It is a dialogue between equals. The codesigned and coproduced product or service is fast becoming reality. The consumer is not king yet, but soon

the consumer will own the company's future through "crowd casting." This will not be limited to intelligence: imagine the company asking teams around the world to solve this or that problem. The company's in-house experts cannot compete with the rest of the world in innovation, design, and technology. A truly global division of labor is coming to us. We have seen only the beginning.

The 3D printer is lowering the entry barrier for products, too. The price is coming down, and the technology is improving fast. These devices are not for mass production, but for personalized products, and when we have 100,000 small 3D printer companies in the world, they will collaborate, and together they will constitute huge factories. The assembly-line structure of industry is coming to an end as the dominant method of production.

THE COMPANY LEVEL

Hierarchies are getting flatter. The CEO is not all-powerful anymore, and employees are not expected to just nod and agree. They want their voices to be heard; they want to be consulted. The trend is clear in nations as well as in companies. The global differences are huge, however. The starting point is not the same, by far. The power distance index developed by Geert Hofstede, the famous expert in global value patterns, indicates that hierarchies are flattest in the Nordic countries. At the same time, these countries are the most individualistic and the most trusting—people there trust one another the most, and they thus need less supervision and control. The steepest hierarchies are in the emerging economies and in the poor countries. The figures tend to illustrate that higher GDP

per person leads to a flatter hierarchy. If this is the case, the hierarchies in the emerging economies will flatten as the countries get richer.

These figures do not tell us what works best. At one extreme, the employee tells the CEO about her negative opinion of the boss—without problems. At the other extreme, the employee does not dare to talk to his boss. Basically, this is about values that change slowly; you cannot establish a flat Danish participative culture in all Asian countries, and vice versa. It is about knowing the culture in which you are operating.

The power of the social media is the all-important transformative, even revolutionary, force. The democratization process will go much faster; expect this decade to become the decade of democracy and self-organizing. When business globalizes, the hierarchies will flatten. That's why the process will move much faster. Knowledge about what is happening in other parts of the world will spread faster than ever. Look at the Nordic countries, learn from them, and adapt their values to your company. It can be done.

The Internet and the "everybody an artist" mindset will unleash an avalanche of creativity and threaten the old hierarchies and the old companies. Remember that the tribe or small village is less innovative than the city. Imagine what the new "global city" can accomplish. The flat society and the flat company are much better adapted to a fast-changing world.

The twenty-first-century company will consist of a number of small, truly independent teams with no global headquarters. Strategy will be decided by the team; budgets will be the only tool that makes the organization one company. The individual teams will be led by common values (the value-driven entity). From bigger and bigger to smaller and smaller: the last century was about big; this century is about small.

A LOOK INSIDE OUR BRAIN

Numerous battles are taking place inside our brain when we buy stuff. The battle between "rational person" and "emotional person" is eternal. It is the theme in films and in the theater. Should we buy the eggs produced by chickens sitting in small cages or those produced by chickens having a more natural life? How do we balance price against animal welfare? Are we ready to pay extra to satisfy our feelings for the animals? Our species is called *Homo sapiens*. We might do better to call ourselves *Homo emotionalis*, or "emotional person." Emotions are the source of many, if not most, of our activities, and our range of emotions is much broader than those of other species, even dogs. The explanation is simple: scientists invented the name. To them, emotions, or feelings, were inferior to knowledge and rationality.

Studies of the brain tell us that, over time, it has developed in three stages for all living creatures. First, we have the *reptilian* brain. Sharks and flies are still only in this stage. Next came the *limbic* brain; this is where our emotions are located. Animals living in groups need to relate to other members of the group, and so social skills are called for. Human beings live in groups. The last stage in the development of the brain is the *cortex*; it is the rational, analytical part of the brain. This is mostly a human phenomenon, but we have all three parts in our head; sometimes they interact in harmony, but now and then they are in conflict: "Should I go for the money or the honor?" (Many films are built around this theme.) The limbic brain and the cortex are fighting inside your mind. Can we measure emotions scientifically? Well, we are working at it.

EMOTIONAL MARKET SEGMENTATION

We can study our need for material products (the need for food, water, chairs, and bookshelves), but the emotional side is more difficult. What is our "need" for a Rolex watch? What is our need for handmade organic soap? Or why do we need or want to watch the latest 007 film with Daniel Craig as James Bond? The need is emotional. In a purely postmaterialist marketplace, how can we segment the emotional "industries"? Emotions cannot be measured, but you can feel them. If you are in love, you know it. Scanning the brain may, just may, prove it—but you do not need proof. (Imagine asking your doctor: "Please, scan my brain; I want to find out if I am in love.") Emotions are complex, and it is difficult, if not impossible, for science to put them into a formula. For business purposes, however, we have to find some classification, some way to identify the emotional spectrum. We must be able to answer when the company puts the crucial question: "This is our new product. Nobody has a material need for it, and we believe it is on the emotional market, but which one? How should we develop our marketing strategy?"

The following formula is an attempt to describe the emotional market. We could go into greater detail, but the biggest challenge is that any product is often on more than one market. Even when we have a classification of only eight different emotional marketplaces, we find that a lot of products will overlap. The lines between these marketplaces are blurred. We have to accept that, especially because the material market is blurred too. Is a certain product—say, a toy—for learning or for play? The way you package and advertise it depends on the answer. Furthermore, most products are on both the materialist and

the emotional market. Sometimes the emotional side of the product is the important one; sometimes it is the materialist aspect that counts for the consumer.

Unless we realize that the emotional aspects are determining more and more consumer choice, we will fail in our efforts. For identifying the emotional appeal we need some tools:

1. *Love and romance.* The market for love and romance is perhaps the largest emotional market. This is not limited to love within couples, but also includes the love among parents, family, and children. Luckily, most of this emotion is outside the marketplace, but cosmetics (beauty) and jewelry are definitely part of it. So is popular music—songs are almost always about love and romance. Most movies have a love story included. A romantic dinner and a romantic holiday are also in this market. So is the toy market: you buy toys because you love the young ones.

2. *Traditions and rituals.* Birthdays, anniversaries, weddings, and religious holidays where gift giving is part of the ritual are important to many companies. Traditions are needed because we want to experience continuity, togetherness, even routine; change is the enemy of tradition. We talk about the "wedding industry." It is growing and includes numerous products and services, from the wedding ring to the cake and the limo for the bride and groom. We need a conglomerate, a one-stop company. As mentioned earlier, the lines are blurred: is a wedding on the love market or the market for tradition and rituals? It is both in this case, but tradition is at the core; few people wish an innovative wedding. In many countries, the Christmas tree is a perfect icon. It is not

exactly practical to have a conifer in the middle of your living room, but it is an essential part of the ritual; don't try not to have one.

3. *Freedom.* You feel free to do what you want. Most of the time we do things because we must, whether we are at work or at home. Sometimes there is an island of freedom in our lives: an hour, a day, or a week when we have no fixed schedule and we feel free. This is a big part of the vacation market; you can swim or sit in the sun, and you can sleep late. It is the visit to the café for a beer or two after work: "Miller Time," as the old and famous brewery ad says. For children, it is when they can play without adult supervision. The summer cottage or the dacha is on this market. It is your House of Freedom. It is the caravan for traveling exactly where you wish to. It is the visit to the theme park or the walk in the forest. The market for freedom is growing as daily life becomes more and more scheduled and more organized.

4. *Giving and receiving care.* It is the health*care* industry. In most countries, healthcare is 10 percent of GDP or more, and that is a lot. It is the nurse, but it is also the hairdresser who caresses your hair. It is the waiter who remembers your preference in drinks. It is the masseur stroking your back. You may think of some shop assistant who helps you with her expertise and doesn't just ask, "How can I help you?" but *does* care and assist. It is good old-fashioned service. Again, the definition is emotional: do you feel cared for, and is the caregiver really giving care? The charity business is definitely in this market. Otherwise you would be stupid if you just threw money on the street. Money for charity is a two-way thing. You have a nice feeling because you have

helped people (or animals or preserving nature) in desperate need, and the needy people are happy to get your donation. It is a win-win situation on the emotional market.

5. *The great answers.* Human beings crave answers to life's most fundamental questions: why are we here; what is the purpose of life; what happens when we die? All societies and cultures have asked these questions, and they always will. Religious institutions deliver answers on this market. Great authors like Shakespeare have contributed a lot of wisdom to help us understand our life as well. Philosophers and thinkers from the ancient Greek ones to today's names have contributed. It is no surprise that the oldest "companies" in the world are the religious institutions. This is an eternal need: pilgrimages are very much alive today in Europe and in Asia. The holy city of Mecca in Saudi Arabia is visited by several million people every year.

6. *Control.* We need to be in control of our life and our day. The slave is not in control; he is controlled by others. This is about predictability, a safe environment, and the absence of fear. You know that if you do one thing, something else will happen. Banks are in the control market—you trust them, and you feel in control. Your savings are safe, or they should be. You drive a car or an SUV and you feel in control. You are the boss. Some electronic devices allow you to feel in control. The automatic toaster, the TV, the automatic lawnmower, or the bicycle will make you feel in control. Products and services should make you feel on top of them—this should be part of the marketing activities. Some products may let you down now and then. The reader will think of some.

7. *Recognition.* A pat on the shoulder says: "You are OK; you have done well." This market includes the nice words to a friend. It means, "I have seen you, you are an individual, and I like these things about you." It is the card (handwritten) for your birthday, it is the nice words to your boss ("You do what you can ☺"). We all need recognition. It is the child showing her drawing: "See what I have done!" In this respect, we are all children. We cannot get enough. It is Andy Warhol's 15 minutes of fame on a small scale, except that it is not 15 minutes, but always. In the marketplace, recognition is often forgotten, and not only in relation to employees. In marketing and sales, many companies have a problem with this. What kind of product has recognition value, we should ask. The answer is obvious: the personal one, the one that says: "This is for you, because I have noticed you, and that's why I am familiar with your taste." It is irresistible.

8. *Change—something new.* We need change now and then. We redecorate our home, we listen to a lecture, and we go to college or to university. We visit a new country or a new restaurant; we learn to draw portraits. We have small changes and big ones. A new piece of furniture is small; extreme sports are extra large. Some people seek change or adventure; other people will normally try to avoid it. How do you find customers for a change product? Talk about the boring routine—the waste of life and experiences and the possibility to fulfill your dreams, small or large.

Again, the lines are blurred. Potatoes may be on the materialist market—ordinary potatoes, that is. But they could also

be on the love market: "My family deserves the best, so I serve fresh, organic potatoes right from the farm nearby." Or is that the care market? It is both.

Water is not on the emotional market—unless it is bottled. A bottle of Perrier is certainly on the recognition market. It says, "Watch what I am having." A film is always on some emotional market. There is no objective reason to watch it; there are only emotional reasons. A Rolex watch can tell you the time—but so can any cheap watch. Why buy it, then? A lot of clever people do, and they do it because they are on the recognition market. Isn't that allowed? Of course it is.

We have deep, strong emotions, and we have shallow ones. You may label the emotional appeal of your products with one or several hearts, just like small, medium, large, or extra large for clothing. The more hearts you have in your product, the higher the price you can ask for it.

The real challenge in the postmaterialist markets (the emotional ones) is that your company may have new and unexpected competitors. The market for romance, cosmetics, flowers, jewelry, and even music are in the same emotional category. The winner is the company that offers the most wanted emotional appeal.

POSTMATERIALISTIC CONSUMERS

The consumers in the mature economies are standing with one foot in the rational, materialistic mindset and the other in the emotional mindset, but gradually they will lift their foot away from the rational mindset and stand with both feet in the emotional one. It is a long, complicated, and, indeed, conflicted period for consumers, for producers, and especially for

the advertising industry. The direction is clear, however, and it is mostly the result of wealth. We can afford to buy with our hearts.

In the old days, emperors could afford objects of prestige, things that told about their power and wealth; they needed to instill admiration and fear in order to stay on their thrones. Today a lot of us have become emperors—we can buy a lot more than we "need." Compared to our grandparents, we are filthy rich. The French emperor Napoleon had all the money he wanted, yet his means of transportation were lousy (he had no car), his doctors were incompetent, and his bathrooms were inferior (no running water). The emperors of Europe were in many ways poor compared to the majority of people in high-income countries today. However, the emperors had more power than any of us, even presidents.

What we see today is arguably the greatest change in the history of *Homo sapiens*. Throughout history, the vast majority of people were preoccupied with survival in a basic physical sense. Would this year's harvest provide food enough to last until the next one? This is still an important question for millions of people on this planet, but they are no longer a majority. Most of us can afford more than basic needs. When our basic needs are satisfied, we turn to demonstrations of our wealth—we buy luxury, "look-how-much-money-I-have" products. This is a natural reaction; we have become rich recently, and we want to tell the world about it. Why shouldn't we? This is Step 1, and it happens in all countries when GDP reaches, say, $15,000 per person. It is still a normal thing in high-income countries. You can afford to buy a Rolls Royce, and so you do it. It is comfortable, but the most important thing is that you are sending a message: I have arrived, I am successful. Napoleon would have owned several golden cars if they had been around 200

years ago. But this is a halfway thing. The real sea change is Step 2. In this step, you are sending messages not about your wealth, but about your values—nonmaterialistic values. This is the big thing, the one we are experiencing in this century. In a thousand years, historians will look back (they always do) and say that the twenty-first century was the most important one in human history, because this was the time when materialism changed to values.

For the company, the result is that the product becomes a by-product and the value, the meaning, the story, becomes the product—this is what you buy. Along with the value comes a product that has a more or less practical purpose. Your friend and you are buying a watch because of the story, the signal, the values it is sending to others. Knowing what time it is—that's a by-product. If you don't understand the logic of this, then learn it by heart. All businesspeople should ask: "What kind of emotional appeal, what kind of meaning, or which story are we selling? What dreams are we fulfilling?" The same applies to services. The banks are selling trust; the travel agency is selling freedom; the fitness center is selling control—find out what your service is really about.

The high-income countries are the pioneers; they are becoming the first postmaterialistic countries in the world. This change will happen gradually. We will still have older people who are buying luxury, but the younger ones have got the message. The middle-income countries (the newly rich ones) will buy luxury products for some time to come. The luxury product industry will gradually move east and south. The low-income countries are still waiting for their Guccis—and Gucci is waiting for them. They will understand each other very well soon.

Lord Keynes, the famous English economist, foresaw this megatrend in his now-famous essay from 1930, "The Economic

Prospects of Our Grandchildren." He wrote: "In a not so distant future, I envision the greatest upheaval that has hitherto occurred in human history. Of course, it will happen gradually, not as a catastrophe. Actually, this development has already begun. What will happen is, quite simply, that the problems of economic necessity will be relieved for an increasing number of classes and groups of individuals." According to Keynes's estimate, this upheaval would take place within 100 years—in other words, by the year 2030. He concluded that the most honored persons will become: "those who can teach us how best to benefit from the hour and the day, these admirable people who know how to enjoy things. Like the lilies of the field."

Those are beautiful words. The lilies of the field—people who can inspire us to improve our quality of life, to laugh, to enjoy beauty—will become the most admired people. Lord Keynes also said that "in the long run we are all dead." This is a proven and deplorable fact, but Keynes's words are alive and will live for centuries. How about this company title: "chief quality of life enhancer"? This is not a joke; the title may not materialize, but the occupation will. Are we talking of artists, philosophers, movie producers, football players, and psychotherapists? Yes, we are. Are we talking about politicians and bankers? Perhaps in the long term, hopefully.

THE SPIRITUAL SUPERMARKET

The core of our emotional life and the center of our emotions could be love, but we might as well say that it is our religious beliefs. They have a prominent place in our value system. St. Augustine, who lived more than 1,500 years ago, said it beautifully: "For what is faith unless it is to believe what you do not

see?" Religion is for the heart; science is for the mind. Science is the answer to "How?"; faith is the answer to "Why?" We say, "This is my belief," and it needs no scientific underpinning. *Homo sapiens* has always believed in some absolute truth. A belief system may have one or more gods or none at all. Religion gives us guidelines; it explains to us the meaning of life, defines the path to the good life, and often tells us what happens when we die. It is the ultimate sense maker for *Homo sapiens*. We need it; we cannot live without it.

The declining belief in authority almost all over the world is at the moment changing religious practice. Religion is moving from the authority of a religious organization to each individual, from religion as an organized hierarchical organization to us; it is individualized religion. This is a slow process; however, it moves like a glacier, slowly but surely. We will still believe in forces stronger than humanity, but this belief is becoming personal: *my* religion.

First, we will see religion practiced in still smaller groups, with less hierarchy and with more room for individual interpretation. The big and rigid organizations will have a greater challenge in meeting the future than the more decentralized and flexible ones. These are steps toward the personal religion. It is faith selected from numerous sources and put together as my beliefs, my guidelines for the good life.

Where do these personal guidelines come from? They come from politics, from business, from wise persons, from different religions, from friends, from social media—and from yourself.

The worldview of religious services is this: in the Americas (plus Poland, Ireland, Nigeria, India, and some Middle Eastern countries), a percentage that is significantly greater than the worldwide average attends a religious service once a week. The figure for the United States is 44 percent; for Mexico,

46 percent; and for India, 42 percent. The Euro-Asian continent is a lot less religious than average, if measured this way. In China, the figure is 9 percent; in South Korea, 14 percent; and in Japan, 3 percent. In Europe, the figure for Russia is 2 percent; for Finland, 4 percent; and for Ukraine, 10 percent. In the West, we pray together; in the East, we do not. This is, of course, a rough summary; it is a painting with big strokes.

Attending a religious service is one thing; belief in God is another. According to a survey by Gallup from 1999 conducted in 60 countries and representing 1.25 billion people, 63 percent say that God is highly important in their life. Some 45 percent say that their God is a person, as against 30 percent who think of God as a "force" or a "spirit." These are not recent figures, but they change very slowly. The most religious people are in West Africa and the Americas. The least religious are from Southeast and East Asia and Europe. The global number of people saying that they do not believe at all is 8 percent. In Europe and Southeast Asia, the percentage of nonbelievers is between 15 and 33.

In the United States and in Europe, available figures suggest that spirituality is not declining, but adherence to organized religion is.

We defined religion as something that you believe in and for which you don't need a proof as you do in science. With this definition, we may consider other beliefs that are of importance to the future of the marketplace.

Puritanism

During the short reign of Oliver Cromwell in England almost 400 years ago, a group of people called the Puritans tried to define the right religious practice. This often involved

forbidding alcohol, tobacco, gambling, and dancing. This is just one example of Puritanism in history; it recurs now and then in all cultures. Just now it is coming back in Western cultures, and it is spreading to the rest of the world. Today it is a belief not about the soul, but about the body—the healthy body. It prescribes how to eat and how to exercise, and it tells you to avoid tobacco, alcohol, and fat. Having a healthy body does not include mental health; actually, it wants us to control our emotions and impulses—to become rational. It is not exactly a philosophy, but the rule of thumb is that if puritans dislike something, it is because it makes life more enjoyable and more fun—it brings happiness. Are the things they dislike dangerous to your health? Yes, they are, but most activities are harmful if they are not enjoyed in moderation. Puritans exclude people (the overweight, the smokers, those who drink sugary soft drinks) from the workplace, from means of transportation, and from public parks. Soon people who don't exercise, who play cards, and who wear expressive clothing may become the target. Some people are good; others are sinners. Perhaps we need somebody to point fingers at?

The Religious Company

Does the religious company exist, and is it somehow replacing organized religion? Yes, if we define religion in a narrow sense. Many companies have a "mission statement" and a "vision," not just a purpose and a goal to reach. Words from religion are entering the boardrooms and the workplace. Some companies have "core values," five to ten rules for the way employees are expected to think, feel, and behave. Call it religion or corporate faith defined by top management. This is an important trend for the future; it is postmaterialistic, as it implies that a salary

is not the sole reason for working. The company of the future will need to have values that both management and employees truly believe in—not a complete belief system, but certain values that are adhered to by all. You will choose to work for this or that company because of its values, not because of the money it will pay you. Start talking about your company's corporate religion. The company of the future may be defined not by industry, but by values. This trend is a strong one, but gradually at least the core values must be discussed and approved by employees as hierarchies flatten.

The Market for Mental Well-Being

More and more people believe that mental well-being is the most serious problem facing humanity just now. Healthcare institutions and governments around the world know it, but they act as if it is a minor issue. Only a fraction of healthcare costs are allocated to mental disorders. Most medical personnel are trained to treat somatic illnesses; mental disorders are not their business. Generally, healthcare costs are growing every year, and adding money to treat mental disorders to the budgets will make this problem even worse. Those who are making the decisions do not want to face reality, but eventually they will have to. When it is not possible to ignore the trends anymore, it will be a revolution, a reappraisal of the way we look at human health. Mental illnesses will be seen as a bigger problem than somatic ones.

Mental disorders are rising, not declining, as one could expect when GDP is growing. We have fine figures for cancer and broken limbs, but for mental diseases, the figures are few and less reliable. The figures from the United States tell us that 25 percent of the adult population suffers from a diagnosable

mental disorder in any given year; that's 57 million people. The figures from the European Union say much the same. Figures from Asia are hard to get, but let us assume that they are comparable.

What is a mental disorder? The major ones are depression, schizophrenia, anxiety disorders, posttraumatic stress disorder, eating disorders, attention deficit hyperactivity disorder (ADHD), and autism. These are the disorders that would get a diagnosis if you asked for it. Add to this the less serious mental disorders, like a period of stress or a minor depression, that just reduce our well-being.

There are two causes for the growing prevalence of mental disorders. The first one is our attention. The taboo is gradually disappearing. We can talk about mental disorders, and the media can write about them. The second cause is modern lifestyles. We can work outside the office, no factory hooter indicates the end of the working day, and no boss will stop you from working too much.

Both causes indicate that the prevalence of mental disorders will continue to grow. Will it grow from 25 percent of the population to 30, 40, or 50 percent? When will it stop? And how can the trend be stopped and reversed? One possibility is treatment; the other is prevention. Better treatment would mean that 50 percent of healthcare personnel would work with mental disorders, and healthcare budgets might reach 15 to 20 percent of GDP (as opposed to 0 percent today). Of course the budgets will have to rise, but prevention is the obvious solution. That is the "nanny state" telling us how to live our lives in a healthy way, both physically and psychically. Imagine government-financed ads saying things such as: "Eight hours of work is enough," "Don't work from home," "Long working hours kill," "Your family is more important than your

work." Governments should do this because mental disorders mean lost working days and reduce the figures for positive well-being.

Well-being is not only about disorders. Just as we have physical fitness, we will have mental fitness. How do you get a better life? Through meditation, religion, positive thinking, studying nature, finding new friends, improving family life, owning a pet—the possibilities are endless. It is a truly future-oriented market.

It is a logical development:

1. The year is 1800. The ability to cure somatic illnesses is limited; only care is available.
2. The year is 2000. More and more somatic illnesses can be cured, and attention is gradually turning toward mental disorders.
3. The year is 2020. Mental disorders are viewed as the new frontier in medical science, the next field to explore. At the same time, mental fitness is recognized as a more or less mature industry, with large companies working globally.
4. The year is 2050. The cure of somatic illnesses is more or less automated, and mental fitness is a major industry.

The role of management is a complicated one. Should we become a "nanny company" and regulate and advise our employees on how to avoid stress and depression? Should we regulate by setting mandatory maximum working hours and creating systems that can detect employees who are working online at home? Should we tell the HR office to make sure that employees are working less and taking more vacations? My guess is that the answers to these important questions

are yes; this is the trend of the future. This will be just like the utility companies—they are selling water or electricity to households, and at the same time they have to tell consumers to save and use less of what they are selling. Employees should be motivated, but not too much. If overweight and smoking are company problems, then stress and other mental disorders are too.

The "I Do Exist" Market

Andy Warhol famously said it: "Everyone will be famous for 15 minutes." Do people really need to enter the public domain to feel that they are somebody, that they exist, and that they are making a difference in the world? Andy Warhol was an artist, not a futurist, but his words are right on target. It started with TV: with talent shows, with *Big Brother*, with reality shows. You enter the public domain, and you may become a semi-celebrity or a full-scale one for a time—or indeed permanently. This was the beginning; the social media are next. Millions of people around the world are on Facebook and other sites on the Internet. Your face is visible for all to see, as are your thoughts, your shopping, and everything else you want to tell about. Then we have a few hundred million bloggers, writing about any subject. It is a fast-moving trend, and it will continue to grow.

Then add to this the hundreds of thousands of people who are contributing to the many wikis and all the unpaid people who give advice to one another about companies, products, and services like banks and travel agencies: which ones are good and which to avoid. We have a new culture of participation, not for money, but to be seen: yes, I do exist; I give advice to companies or to other consumers. It gives me a feeling of

empowerment. I am somebody; I contribute beyond my family and friends.

How will this trend develop in, say, 10 years? Clearly, this is only the beginning. We have many different interests: political, social, personal, and commercial. All sorts of issues are put on the Internet, and it is important that these virtual communities be able to find each other. This is most often not the case today. In 10 years' time, let us expect that there will be 500 to 10,000 major communities. Each will have its own interests or theme, from a group criticizing or helping Walmart to those fascinated by fly fishing. Most groups will be more or less global; they will be interest-based, not based on geography. These sites will become an invaluable source of information for companies and public institutions. Some companies may be able to influence the sites; others will only be able to study trends and values as they develop. Smart companies will create these communities and get all the interested parties to join their sites. There will be fierce competition, but the trend is winner take all. Imagine the site for small airplanes. Owners, pilots, and other enthusiasts will share their experiences, and the producers will look into the site and will want to influence what happens. Or, more likely, they will ask questions and ask people to assist them. Studying the market will become easier and cheaper. But of course, whether you as a company take part or not, the market is becoming a lot more transparent. What about the journalists writing for professional magazines about aviation? They may own the site.

What about the 15 minutes of fame—the celebrity industry? A number of celebrity or semicelebrity sites will morph into one gigantic "15 minutes or more" site. Who will run it? The companies with big search engines will run the show—and a show it is. As in aviation, the income will come from ads, as it

does today, and perhaps from the possibility of buying market information and becoming part of this or that famous person's life through an offer of clothing or jewelry. It will become one of the most valuable sites on the planet, with billions of visitors. People will be able to follow the lives of top celebrities and the not so famous. And it will be possible to rate the popularity of each celebrity—from number 1 to number 2 million, just as Amazon is doing today with books, except that it will be measured not by sales, but by unique visitors and friends.

The experts, the professors, and the analytic people may take part in these global agoras, but it is more likely that they will watch from the sidelines and get a thousand ideas from the public—from you and me. Creativity is not for the experts only.

I would say that every company should ask itself one question: how can we make every individual customer feel important, valued, and empowered? If you don't come up with a good answer, you may have a problem in the near future.

Thanks to the Internet, the "silent majority" is not silent anymore. It has a voice, and it will speak louder and louder. It is a clever idea to listen carefully. When people have a lot of knowledge and do not feel the same respect for authorities that they once did, they don't want to be bullied by companies and institutions. We may be simply a voter now and then, a passive consumer who is buying McDonald's burgers because "I'm lovin' it." At the same time, we feel empowered by the fact that we have a voice, we are somebody. A contributor to Wikipedia, a participant in a talent show, a blogger telling us which tablet is best—the possibilities are endless; why not take part yourself? Actually, it is old Maslow helping us again. The top of the ladder is "self-actualization." This is what we are about to do, take the next step.

FROM DARK TO LIGHT

Our species is an outdoors one; we were not created to sit in some office and look at a screen, sip coffee, and write e-mails. Once, everything we needed in life was outside: the food, the animals, the vegetables. It looks as if we are taking back our past; we are returning to it. The Western trend in living is obvious: we are moving the living space out into the garden, and we are moving the garden into the house. The cod is on your grill, yes, but the complete outdoor kitchen is next. Do we need an outdoor kitchen? No, of course not, we have one inside, but it gives us a sense of freedom; we are closer to our roots. Our homes are getting greener, with more nature inside. The next step will be a small artificial creek somewhere near the fireplace (just in case).

City life is nice, but it's artificial. You can make a living from sitting at a desk. It is strange, but true. You can make money without using your muscles today, but your muscles still need exercise. That is why we see people running in the streets and parks, and they are not busy or running away from somebody. They are just running for fun and because their bodies need it. We have fitness centers, but outside is seen as the better, more genuine solution.

We are getting back to nature: mountain climbing, trekking, water sports, skiing, surfing, whitewater rafting, bungee jumping, golf, horseback riding. In sports, outdoors is the trend. Our bodies have retired from work, but not from exercising—we need it. And we need to escape the city and enjoy the freedom of nature. Thirty years ago, vacation tourism was about relaxing from the daily routine; today it is about new experiences, and most of it concerns nature and unspoiled places.

Our products are changing from nice and sleek to raw. What does that mean? A mountain bike is raw, it is sturdy, and it tells a story about its owner: he must be an outdoors person. The SUV (sports utility vehicle) or the off-road vehicle is raw, too. The owner must be a raw outdoors person. She is just in town to buy provisions before returning to the old mountain cottage with lots of deer and an occasional grizzly bear—but nothing that would scare her. Most motorcycles are raw, too, and the tools you buy in the hardware store must be raw—not for hobbyists, but the tools a real craftsman would use. It's the same with most of the tools in the kitchen.

Well, this is mostly a trend for high-income countries; it is postmaterialistic. Still, it is a megatrend because at some time in the future, it will become a global trend. When most people live in cities and work at a desk, they will need exercise and nature.

Now it gets complicated. The workplace is changing too; it is becoming more open and more transparent, with more glass and more open space. Why? It is the same trend, but the reasons are different. The idea is better control (you can watch what the boss and your colleagues are doing), while at the same time conveying the impression of less hierarchy—we are all sitting in the same office, aren't we? It is also more transparent from outside; we can see people sitting inside and working. The employees have the impression that they are connected to the real world, that they are close to the customers. Glass, glass, and more glass is the obvious solution for the architects.

We like the outdoors, yes, but we like it during our leisure time. It is about our vacations. We don't want to live in the countryside permanently. We prefer the city, where we are close to work and to other people. That is OK, but soon we will have the megacities on the one hand and the almost depopulated

rural areas on the other. This is a lack of balance, and in the process we will see the countryside getting poorer and poorer, with lots of jobs being lost and house prices coming down. This process has begun, and it will continue for many years to come. The outdoors trend will not go away; it could be supplemented by interest in "mental fitness," but that too will often require the calm and unspoiled serenity of nature. Rural development programs will be introduced to alleviate the situation, but at best, they will only delay the process. We have to do something new to avoid this development. Ideas are called for.

THE HAPPINESS MARKET: THE RISE AND FALL OF GDP

The easiest way to measure happiness is simply to ask people: "On a scale of one to ten, all in all, how happy do you feel?" Or you could ask: "Are you thriving, struggling, or suffering?" It is a subjective thing. Just as you may ask your employees how they like their work, nations are beginning to ask their citizens, the voters, how they feel. GDP is the traditional yardstick for a nation's success, but in the rich countries, GDP growth does not increase people's happiness. As GDP grows worldwide and more and more countries reach the point where more GDP does not increase happiness, we need a new yardstick. In the poor parts of the world, the correlation is still good, however; economic growth increases happiness. Forward-looking international institutions are already measuring happiness or quality of life; we have Gallup, World Values Survey, and Eurobarometer measures today, and many national projects will be launched soon. Expect GDP to be supplemented by these new "soft" figures during the next 10 years.

Look at a bottle and ask: where is the bottleneck? The obvious answer is, at the top. The same is true for politicians; they are the bottleneck today. They fear new things. Several studies are initiated, but with a few exceptions, our politicians ignore the results. Gradually, the voters will compel them to use these studies, and they will find that just asking a few questions does not provide a reliable tool for policy making. You have to dig deeper. Happiness is about emotions, and you will have to address those emotions, like love, care, recognition, and rituals. Most studies indicate that relationships are the most important. Trust and tolerance are equally important. You have to open the concept of happiness and identify its components. Perhaps in 15 years we will have just as many experts studying emotional well-being as we have economists today.

For businesses, the relevant question to ask is this: how can our products enhance the happiness of consumers? Water is water, isn't it? No, it is not. You have tap water and bottled water. It is essentially the same product, but the prices are definitely not the same. If such a simple product as water can be provided with an emotional appeal, all products can be given one. Does branded water make customers happier? Yes, that is why they are willing to pay more for it. How? It can give them recognition, a feeling of identity: "look at what I am drinking, I am a sophisticated and healthy person."

This story could be true: Swedish bottled water (Ramlösa) is sold in Italy, and Italian bottled water (Pellegrino) is sold in Sweden. It is bottled in the respective countries and transported a long way. Sometimes the truck drivers will pass each other on some German road, one northbound with Italian water, and one southbound with Swedish water. They will nod to each other and laugh. They have got a valuable insight into human nature. This is the experience economy, the dream

society trend. I could tell you about numerous branded products, but as I said, if it works for water, it will work for any product or service. It is the future.

Disney is a happiness company. It makes people happy; they visit Disney World and go to Disney movies. It is part of the entertainment industry. Happiness is fine, but that's just one emotional appeal. With a horror movie, you sit and watch something terrible happen, and you may even close your eyes—you don't want to watch the scene where she falls off the cliff. You pay gladly to be scared stiff. Why? You have a chance to exercise your emotions without risking your life. The emotional market is full of opportunities that are waiting to be discovered.

My advice is to ask what kind of emotional appeal your product has. If the answer is none, you are in a commodity market; you are most likely engaged in fierce price competition. Add emotions, add a story, and make your product unique.

This century is about exercising "the pursuit of happiness." It was written into the U.S. Declaration of Independence in 1776 as one of the inalienable human rights. It ought to be written into every national constitution.

How We Will Produce and How We Will Consume

HOW WE WILL PRODUCE AND CONSUME—THE RELATIONSHIP

In the good old days, it was easy: we consumed what we produced. Even the farmhouse and the furniture were most often built by the farmer's family and employees, with the neighbors' help. Most of the economic growth since that time can be explained by just three trends:

1. *Division of labor and specialization.* Most of us are specialists; we are educated to do one job, whether it be accounting or sales, and we know next to nothing about, say, a construction worker's job. It would be a disaster if we switched jobs.
2. *Globalization.* Thanks to globalization, the specialization today is worldwide. The value chain from producer

to consumer has become very long. Nearly half of the products in the open Nordic countries come from another country.

3. *Power.* Thanks to oil, coal, and other sources of energy, humanity today has immensely more power, more forces other than human muscles that can be used to produce stuff. At the same time, innovation and new technology have automated things that were once done by human labor; the machines have taken over.

The hunter/gatherer would starve and most likely die if he lost one of his five senses. Today, for working purposes, many people use only their eyes, their voice, and their brain (and their ears if they listen); the other senses are reserved for leisure activities. The machines, both the mechanical ones and the electronic ones, have taken over; they have become our humble slaves, and they don't complain. Some of these slaves are quite clever; they have begun to take over big parts of our memory and even our ability to reason. Will the brain, too, in some distant future, not be needed in the workplace anymore? Will the clever robots be putting in the long hours in the office, while we use our brains for fun only? (Will there be a robot lawyer who, like a chess computer, can win any case in the courtroom?) We have already seen the beginning of this future.

Consumption in the old days was easy, too. Food, drink, a bed, and not much else—these were the material necessities for a decent life. Our needs were basic and easy to forecast. Less than a hundred years ago, 50 percent of our income would have been spent on food and drink even in the rich parts of the world; today it is as little as 15 percent.

Thanks to automation, the future belongs to services. In high-income countries, 75 percent of GDP is generated from

services. By services, we mean government and community services, business services like banking and insurance, education, healthcare, retail, communication, tourism, and personal services. Services are the last activity that has not been fully automated. We need people, not machines, as politicians, civil servants, nurses, and motivational speakers. Or do we? Robots may replace the surgeon and even the nurse, but we still don't have a robot that can give care and show compassion (although it is on its way). When we order our tickets and products on the Internet, the salesclerk loses her job. Just as machines took over the task of producing cars, electronic devices will take over a growing part of the service industries. In 10 years' time, jobs in banks and in government will be a lot more automated. As a customer or a citizen, you will have to contact an electronic device, not a human being. What can be automated and what cannot? Almost all services can be automated, but the question is, which jobs do we want to remain unautomated in order to feel human?

Agriculture and fisheries are contributing just 1 percent to GDP in high-income countries, and very few people are employed in farming because so much of it has been automated—the machines do the work. This is almost the end of the line for farm jobs. Still, farms provide us with an abundance of food, actually more than when the farmer was working with his hands and the farmer's wife was tending the kitchen, the chickens, and the farmer himself.

Manufacturing contributes just 16 percent to GDP in high-income countries. Manufacturing involves the factories that produce shoes, textiles, cars, machinery, and chemicals. The factory floor is more or less unpopulated; the workers that are still employed are mostly supervising the processes, and automation is still continuing. Again, thanks to automation, the

factory produces a lot more than it did when the assembly line was crowded with workers.

Industry (other than manufacturing) contributes approximately 9 percent to GDP. Industry refers to construction, mining, oil and gas, electricity, and water.

To sum up, in a rich country, three-quarters of GDP comes from services. The remaining 25 percent comes from industry, manufacturing, and agriculture. The vast majority of the workforce works with computers and paper and communicates with other people. This is the fruit of automation, specialization, and the long value chain. It is a future that will come to the emerging economies sooner or later. When they reach a GDP per capita of, say, $40,000, we can assume that they will have the same structure of production as the high-income countries have today.

The structural transformation from manufacturing to services is slow; it changes only 2 to 4 percent per decade. This is a blessing, because it is a fundamental change for society and especially for individuals; they will have to change jobs, learn new skills, and move to a new city. Can we imagine a society with 95 percent of its people employed in the service sector? If we assume that the growth in services will continue at the same rate as in the past, then 95 percent of GDP will come from services by 2040, and the same percentage of people will be employed in service industries.

If our three trends work in the same way in the future (and most likely they will), the 2 to 4 percent structural change per decade has enormous implications. Low-skilled work will be replaced by higher-skilled work, increased specialization will require skills that are deeper and narrower (you know more about less), and the global value chain will become even longer and more complicated. The growth industries are

education, healthcare, and research and development, and automation of these services will happen, too. The longer value chain tells us that transportation is a global growth industry as well.

Will work disappear thanks to the three trends? If everything is becoming automated, then the machines can reproduce (robots can produce robots), and sensors can replace our eyes and brains. The answer is simple: if this were true, then a large part of the population in the rich part of the world would already be unemployed. Let me illustrate what is happening with a compressed story of one man's working life. He moves to new jobs, jobs that did not exist before:

- Harry starts as a farmhand. The farmer buys machines, so he is not needed.
- He moves to town and works on an assembly line. Either it gets robots or the factory is moved to a low-cost country.
- He gets a job as a salesclerk, but the cash registers are automated.
- He gets a job as a security guard, but the company buys sensors and cameras.
- He goes to college and gets a job as a designer, or he works with computer games.
- Harry retires after a long work life.

Harry has been chased by our three trends all his working life, mostly by automation, but also by specialization. Of course, this story will cover more than one lifetime, but if we include just two or three generations of Harrys, it is true for most people in the rich part of the world, and it is on its way in the emerging economies.

Demand will always create new jobs. During recessions, unemployment is unavoidable, but in the long term, demand will create jobs. The structure of the economy is changing; this has been called *creative destruction*—new jobs replace the ones that disappear. It starts with the need-driven jobs and ends with a demand for what most of us will call play, or jobs that provide us with fun as well as money. Professional sports is one example. Not all of us can get work in sports, but perhaps we can get work as providers of other entertainment, as experience producers, or as psychotherapists, PR people, marketing people, or nature coaches. The demand is endless.

The only way to reduce the workforce and put most of us on eternal vacation would be to stop demand. No new activities must come along: no 3D TV, no smartphones, no such thing as new technology. People would have to just replace what they have with new similar items. That would stop GDP from growing—it would stay the same. Will it happen? Yes, when we have two Tuesdays in one week. Work is here to stay, as is production, but increasingly it will look like play. After all, when we sit in the office or have a meeting, it would look like play to our forefathers. They would think we were having a good time and producing nothing. Can sipping coffee, talking, and laughing be work? "No way; real work is something you do with your hands, that much I know," my grandfather would tell me.

The future of consumption can be illustrated with Mrs. Mary's history from 1820 to 2020 in six steps, six patterns of consumption. Mrs. Mary and her family happen to live in the United Kingdom, near London.

1. 1820. The first step is survival. Mary and her family probably live in the countryside, on a family farm. Their

goal is making their harvest last until the next season. Famine is always a possibility. They consume what they produce and buy just a few things from outside, from the marketplace.

2. 1880. The next step is surplus. Mrs. Mary and her family can now afford to buy more clothes than they need to keep them warm. They will have more rooms than they use every day, and they may have money in the bank for a rainy day (or rather for the opposite, a drought).

3. 1920. The next step is convenience. They will buy electricity and water closets; they will buy train tickets. Life has become a lot easier. Instead of farm production, they buy a lot from the local retailer—they have become modern consumers.

4. 1980. Now Mrs. Mary and her family have moved to the city. They can buy a radio, a TV, and a telephone—and later a mobile phone. They will buy a small car, and vacations abroad are within reach. Their children may go to college.

5. 2005. The next step is luxury. By now Mrs. Mary and her family can buy more than they "need." They will buy a big car. Shopping is a lifestyle; they buy branded products in the supermarket and at Harrods in London. Occasionally they go to a fine restaurant. Their yearly vacation moves from the coasts of the Mediterranean to the Pacific coasts.

6. 2020. The last step is emotion-driven consumption, or self-actualization. If the reader thinks that this family's history looks like Maslow's hierarchy of needs, yes, it is the same, although in more concrete words. The family has reached the top of the hierarchy: self-actualization.

The family members may now prefer organic products; they may visit farmer's markets on Saturday afternoon. Their car must reflect their lifestyle, and they will talk about their quality of life and well-being. They will donate to charity and try to achieve a better work-family balance. The family will look down on luxury as being over the top and too materialistic. It has reached the postmaterialistic level.

Is there a seventh step at some time in the future? No. By definition, there is nothing beyond postmaterialism (other than a return to materialism). We are increasingly living in an emotion-driven society; we consume in order to satisfy our feelings, not just our stomachs. You go to a restaurant because you are hungry, but the real issue is emotional. The food and drink must appeal to our senses; having enough to eat is a by-product. In the old days, if you were asked: "Who are you?," the answer would be about one's family; today the answer would be what you do for a living. In the future, the answer will be your lifestyle: "I am a car buff," "I am a bird-watcher," "I am a computer gamer," and so on. This has begun; look at the wide variety of magazines, paper or online. Each of them reflects a certain lifestyle and a certain way to use your money. The lucky ones are those whose lifestyle is the same as what they do for a living.

Don't forget that even if some of us buy more therapy, more alternative treatments, and more spirituality, we still need stuff. Furthermore, not all of us will become more spiritual; some will prefer car racing and extreme sports. Whatever we choose, it is all about stuff plus emotion. Your mobile phone is not primarily a communication tool; it is mostly a lifestyle statement. The design and color is a statement; it is a message that is

supposed to tell others who you are as a person. We buy products for, say, 50 percent rational reasons and 50 percent as an individual statement. Gradually, what we are really paying for will become the emotional aspect of the product: our choices will be 99 percent emotional and 1 percent rational.

THE SELF-ORGANIZING SOCIETY

Societies in all countries started as decentralized, fragmented, loosely connected entities with a minimum of central authority. The rulers would do some tax collection, but local headmen could do as they pleased. Since then, centralization has taken place, and the public sector and the number of rules and regulations have exploded. Authorities are organizing our lives today; they tell us how to behave and what to do. Our societies have become hierarchical. The governments are claiming that they can create jobs, make schools and universities better, and ensure better healthcare. Can they do that? Up until now, it has looked as if they are doing it. That means that institutions like schools, whether private or public, cannot do anything unless the authority to do it comes from above. This situation won't last. We can expect people to organize without regard for authorities: the self-organizing society. Don't look to government for your future; do something yourself. The role of government will become much smaller; it will provide some basic services, and generally, it will be seen as a mere helper, not a ruler. The social hierarchy will flatten because more and more citizens will feel empowered to act on their own. This transformation will unleash a lot of dreams and make for a happier society. Many countries in the emerging economies have a large private sector and fewer rules; in the West, it is the

opposite: a large public sector and a small private one. Let us assume that the private sector will play an increasing role in the West and a decreasing role in the East.

THE US-ME INDUSTRY

Imagine a visit to a toy shop called Build-a-Bear. It sells what it says: mass-customized bears for children. The child gets a personal bear with its own name and birth certificate. It's an assembly line, and the children are the "workers"—they select what suits their own taste. It is still Us (Build-a-Bear), but it is also Me (the smiling child). The Us-Me industry is on its way to a company near you. When these children grow up, they will not buy mass-produced stuff. The toy market is one small example. Consumer electronics is another. It is still a Nokia or a Samsung cell phone, but it will soon become personalized. It will have your message on the cover—a picture, some words, or some design that is just for you. You do the individualization in the shop on its computer, and you click "print." The list of possibilities is long: cars, bicycles, soft drinks, beer, watches, ties, TV, and all products for the kitchen, the bedroom, and the bathroom. Your online newspaper and magazine will have just the news you want. The stamps and postcards you buy will have your own picture. Your clothing and your shoes will be personalized; they are still Nike or Puma, but they will be your Puma.

This is happening for two reasons. First, new technology is the enabler—sometimes the company or retailer uses it; sometimes you do it yourself. Second, but equally important, in a market where personal products are becoming available, consumers want it. You can tell the world, or at least your friends,

who you are: I am somebody, an individual with his own taste, but I am still a member of this or that group. The Puma and me. The signals you are sending to the world are a combination of the products you own. They reflect your lifestyle. Yesterday, you wanted just the group portrait, the Us-Us industry; today, you want the group portrait, but with yourself as an important part of the portrait. Gradually the Puma may get smaller and the Me will grow in size. There is a third and obvious reason: more and more consumers are willing to pay the slightly higher price for personalization.

This trend fits well with the transformation from mass marketing to personal marketing. Even strong brands like Apple will join; you are still an Apple person, but you are an individual, too. You can demonstrate just *how* you are an Apple fan.

We are living in a globalized world, but with a lot of different values and cultures, and they will not disappear in our lifetime, if they ever do. Individualization is the key to mass marketing your product anywhere in the world as long as the consumer has a personal choice. The personalization can be done either in production or at the retailer, but the future may be for the customer's doing it herself—online, using your company's software.

THE "HANDMADE" INDUSTRY IS GROWING

We are slowly returning to the era before the Industrial Revolution, before mass production. It is a nostalgic trip, but it is not only that. We want products that were made with passion; a person made them with his own hands. They were made according to an old tradition or because the craftsperson

wanted them to be like this. They are personal; they have a soul; they are products with a heart. The craft breweries make beer this way because they believe it should taste like this. In Asia, vodka, sake, and soju are popular drinks with a lot of traditions, and old family recipes are waiting to be rediscovered. It will happen soon. The soap maker chooses her ingredients according to her ideas. And she knows her craft in all stages of the production, and she tells her customers about it: the handmade soap.

The handmade industry is a reaction to cold, impersonal production. You don't know how and where something is produced, and the ads are hard to believe in. You may think it is made for profit only. It does not cost a lot, however, and the quality is OK, no problem.

The mass-production market and the handmade market will coexist nicely—both will have their customers. But the handmade industry is emerging and getting its small but growing share of the market. Each "handmade" company has to stay small; otherwise it is entering mass production without the scale and knowhow to compete on the supermarket shelves. It is the market for entrepreneurs, those that are under the radar right now in business magazines. They are doing it for money, but basically they are doing it because they love their craft.

Only a few industries have survived the depersonalizing effect of the Industrial Revolution. Art is one of them. We still buy paintings, sculptures, novels, music, and films because they are created by a person, someone with a message and a passion. A painting is not a real painting unless you know who created it. A work of art is personal. The designers may mass-produce their designs, but still the passion is coming through, more or less. Today many restaurants have a chef whose name is known; your meal is a personal product made with pride.

Almost all products for consumers can be made by hand. Bicycles, clothes, furniture, motorcycles, jewelry, and carpets—the list is long. We are rediscovering the old crafts: the carpenter, the smith, the cabinetmaker, and the shipbuilder.

What about handmade chicken? Yes, you can buy free-range chickens from a traditional farm. They are raised by the farmer (or, more likely, by the farmer's wife), and the chickens have had a pleasant life until it was time to market them. Is this about nostalgia and animal welfare? Yes, indeed, but there is a passionate market for it. You know where and how the product is produced. You can get hand-picked apples from this farm and cheese from free-range goats from that farm. As a consumer, you feel that this is local; this is genuine; this has got a story along with the product.

Sometimes the story is false, however. Some mass-produced food products are marketed as if they came from some old-fashioned farm. The tomatoes are grown by this elderly farmer, and his wife has blended the tomato sauce in her kitchen according to some old secret recipe passed on from generation to generation—or so the label on the product may claim. The reality is, of course, different. It may be legal to tell false stories, but it proves that the market for handmade products (the real ones) answers our dreams.

An iPad and a smartphone are not part of our body (yet), but they are part of our soul. However, they may not reflect your style, like a pair of jeans in the wrong color. We want to reclaim our soul. We want to become masters of our lives again. Still, we need the devices in our daily life. How can these two conflicting needs be reconciled? We can design the cabinets in our image, to our own taste—they must like us. A wooden cabinet or a retro one is a possibility. The "steam punk" movement is producing computer cabinets as if they

were designed by craftsmen from the Victorian era. This was the age of steam and coal; the cabinets have a lot of brass and pipes.

THE UNDER-THE-RADAR MARKET

Consider the brewing industry. It used to be for the big players only; these players got fewer and bigger all the time, and they still do. The new trend started in the United States with the small craft breweries, and it is highly contagious—more and more cities around the world have a local craft brewery. These breweries are small, and if they are to be able to make money, they have to stay small; they must not enter the supermarket shelves. The clever ones know that, and there are many clever ones. Craft breweries may not end up dominating the world markets (even in 20 years), but their collective share of the market is growing. In the United States, their share of revenue today is 10 percent and still growing. They sell premium beer with a story, and the consumers like the stories and are willing to pay extra for the beer.

The business guru Chris Anderson became famous (and rightly so) when he launched his "long tail" article in *Wired* magazine in 2004; subsequently he made it into a book. When you can cut the cost of printing, storage, and distribution by publishing online, you open up a huge market for books, music, and magazines. Publishers run a very small risk by selling online. That's why Mr. Anderson claims that the industry will make more money from books for niche markets. The blockbusters will still exist, but they are not vital for the publishers' income any longer. The message is this: thousands of new authors and artists will get access to the market. They may

not make a lot of money, but that may not be the reason for their activity. On the other hand, they may be lucky. The barriers to entry into this market has been lowered permanently. The same thing applies to newspapers.

New technology is helping people who dream about making a film. The cost of equipment has come down. In some not too distant future, you will be able to compete with the studios—you will need only talent. Consumers will get their film online and watch it from their sofa. For the blockbusters, they will go to the cinema and watch them in 3D.

Let us go back to products. The 3D printer can print any product, like a vase, a sculpture, or a cell phone cover. It is the real thing; it is in three dimensions. Becoming a famous designer has been something for the few, but that is not so any more (perhaps not world famous, but less will do). The price of these printers is coming down; in less than 10 years, a lot of households will own one. Again, the barriers to entry will be lowered. Today a lot of creativity is lost because of the centralized structure of the industry, but it will be broken down.

The last big consumer product where economies of scale really count, the car, is another example. You need at least 200,000 cars per year per assembly line to survive on the mass market—and it is massive, with 70 million vehicles sold every year. The mass market is shrinking, just like that in any other industry. The new entrepreneurs will turn your Hyundai or Ford into your personal car, not another mass-market product. The car will tell your friends, your family, and everybody else who you are. After some paintwork and some bodywork, it is your special car. The same is happening with bicycles; they are designed and assembled just for you, to your taste and to your body. The mass-production car is just the raw material for the real product.

In IT, we will see a lot of apps and even operating systems invented not by the big companies, but by small teenage companies. By the way, this was how it all started 100 years ago: with numerous small companies. They grew bigger and bigger, but now the era of small companies is back again.

The most important under-the-radar industry, however, is the mental one. The wellness market is on its way. Treatment of diseases of the body (somatic illnesses) is a huge global industry today, but treatment of the mind is the next big thing. This is not limited to treatment for depression and other mental diseases, but also includes wellness, or feeling better and having a more balanced life. Most companies in this market are small businesses operated mainly by women. But, again, we see a lot of them today under the radar, and the industry is growing fast. Sometime this century, its collective revenues may equal that of hospitals. The need for wellness is obvious; just study the happiness index or the low satisfaction with life figures.

Looking for these businesses is easy; it does not require a lot of thinking, just some knowledge of history. At the dawn of the last century, there were more than 100 car producers in the United States alone, most of them producing for a local or regional market. Consider the beer market: every town had its own brewery and even its own bank. Then came centralization (mergers and acquisitions), and we ended up with a few more or less global producers. This is not the end of the story, however. We forgot the teenagers. The business landscape 10 years from now will have a lot of small companies eating away the market share and profit of the big ones. They will still be big, but we will have two kinds of businesses: the big grown-ups and the teenagers. We may call it the new decentralization. But remember, the teenagers (most of them) have to stay small in order to survive; their overall importance is in their

number, not their size. The trend is solid because it is based on structural changes that will get stronger over time. One is individualization; we want personalized products instead of the set menu. Growing wealth will ensure its future. The other one is IT: the Internet and lower prices for electronic products. And remember, when more and more people reach Maslow's top level, self-actualization, their motives for doing something will more often not be profit. They will do things because they want to. That will be a hard lesson to learn for a lot of people who were educated in the past.

THE E-COMMERCE REVOLUTION

Imagine lots of empty shops on Main Street in 10 years. "Closed because of e-commerce" the signs will tell us. Is it likely? We have had nice shop windows to look at for more than 100 years—is it over? This is a possibility, even though most retail companies are selling both offline and online, or perhaps they are converting the shop into a showroom. The e-commerce revolution has started, but we haven't seen the end of it.

Two billion people (out of seven billion) on this globe have access to the Internet today, and the figure is growing fast. One billion, or 50 percent of those with Internet access, have done Internet shopping. This figure is growing by between 10 and 20 percent every year. When you have Internet access, then you buy online. In many countries, more than 90 percent of Internet users have shopped online. South Korea is number one with 99 percent. In the United States, the United Kingdom, Germany, and Japan, nearly all Internet users (more than 90 percent of them) buy online.

The most popular items are books; clothing, accessories, and shoes; videos and DVDs; games; airline tickets; and electronic equipment. New products are added to the list every day.

As one would expect, reliable figures for global e-commerce revenue are hard, if not impossible, to find. For the top 100 retailers worldwide, online shopping accounts for just 6 to 7 percent of their total revenue, but that is still more than $100 billion. Add to this the amount for Amazon, the mother of all online shops ($25 billion), and then consider all the rest. It is likely that total online shopping revenue has yet to match Walmart's total revenue of $400 billion. We cannot be sure, however, and what we are looking for is not today but the future. How will online shopping develop? Should shops fear the future if they are not selling online? Can we imagine that an online shop some day will overtake Walmart as the biggest retailer in the world? Yes, it is likely.

Note that nearly all people in the high-income countries with Internet access buy online. It is a new way of buying, and it takes time to get accustomed to it. A lot of product development takes place today on companies' home pages, whether through trustworthy peer reviews or better product descriptions. When a friend of yours has tried something, then it is OK for you, too. Normally, the price will be lower for products bought online, and you can compare prices easily on the Internet. Clothing is probably bought online because of the lower prices. Selling books, magazines, newspapers, videos, music, and tickets online without the physical product is Internet shopping as well; it's a specialized industry that will probably be dominated by a few big companies. A visit to the bank? The branches on the street corners will disappear in 10 years. You will transfer money via your smartphone. Your visit to a public office? Don't expect to meet a real living person.

Physical shops need more employees, and they pay rent; their expenses will rise more than those for online shopping, which uses fewer people and has the potential for higher productivity. Can we buy food online? Yes, it is likely. The conclusion is clear: a lot of space at ground level in cities will be empty 10 years from now. The shop as we have known it for more than a hundred years is an endangered species—unless retailers reinvent themselves.

THE SHOP AS THEATER

The main problem is not the relationship between online and offline; it is the relationship between the customer and the shop. Retailers can reverse the trend if they have imagination and creativity. In the old days, you went to the store because you needed a certain product. You needed shoes, so you bought shoes. Today shopping is becoming part of our leisure time. It is like going to the theater to watch and perhaps find a role you want to play. Your products are part of your identity, your part in life's great theater. You may want to buy into this specific role and become this actor, or you are looking for a new role to change your identity in a small way (or in a big way). The customer is asking: "Who am I? Whom do I wish to become tonight or tomorrow?" You get inspiration in the store. The store will become an inspiration provider, a dream enabler.

Another reason for shopping comes right from our hunter/gatherer ancestors. What kind of animal or fruit can I bring home to my tribe/family today? I can tell them about the killing: I got a good and clever bargain; I paid only this much; I am a good hunter/gatherer. Discount is certainly part of the future because it is still a role you want to play.

These are good reasons to rethink your store, but the challenge from e-commerce will push you in the same direction. Identity buying or bargain hunting must be more fulfilling than ordering online.

How do you turn your store into a theater? We have already seen some innovations. A bookshop with a café or a café with books is a possibility. A food store with a restaurant is another. A sports store could have an area to test the equipment. Cinemas will sell CDs, and you may blend your very own fragrances in the store. Or you may have a chance to chat with the producers, and perhaps give some advice; this is called empowerment. As a store owner, you need a director to tell your story, to turn the shop into a theater. Perhaps you can be your own director— write your own script and turn the salesclerks into casters. They will suggest exciting roles for the customers (the actors).

If you ask: "What are we offering in our store?," one answer could be cosmetics; another and more future-oriented answer would be "love and romance." In that case, your store may add clothing, footwear, and accessories to its product line. Perhaps you might even add things for the wedding, like rings and wedding gowns. The assumption is, of course, that what the customer "needs" is an emotional thing, not a practical one.

Department stores may even have a renaissance if they can offer products and services that cover most of our emotional needs. The theme of the second floor would be *freedom* (beer and wine, entertainment, and fun). That of the third floor would be *control* (fitness equipment, health food, and books on losing weight). The fourth floor would offer the *great answers* (books on and products connected with religion and spirituality—all products that offer answers to life's big questions). On the ground floor you would find products for the hunter/gatherer—the bargain hunter.

THE SHOP AS FACTORY

The traditional store is the last leg in the value chain. Before the consumer buys the product, we have the creator, the producer, the marketer, and the logistics. The consumer consumes what the long line of companies in the value chain offers. The trend of the future is a store where the consumer becomes the creator. The consumer is creating and producing at the same time. The obvious example is the 3D printer store. Amateur artists visit, create, and produce; they watch what others are doing; and they become a club, a community of passion for creating objects of art. A painters' club is another possibility.

A place where members can brew their own beer or whisky is perhaps more difficult to organize, but it can be done—even legally. There could be a "sweatshop" where you can come and create and make your own clothing, selected from fabric available at the shop and with friendly advice from experts. Again, you get inspiration and friends with the same interest—another community. The participatory store is the answer.

This new type of store may even turn into the much-talked-about "third place," the one between home and work. The old London clubs were that for elderly gentlemen, who would have a clever conversation while smoking a cigar and sipping a drink—they would share the same interests in business, politics, and mistresses. The modern club or third place will be for the creators, but also for the sports fans (visit your club, watch videos, and select your own team—you are the manager), the movie fans (the *Avatar* or *Star Wars* store), and the computer games nerds. The huge community of computer games people needs a common place to meet other fans; it is fast becoming the new café with a billiard table, except that you play games

instead of billiards. With big 3D screens and ever more exciting games, it is a winner.

Retail is becoming one of the most exciting, innovative, and fast-growing industries in business.

THE ONE-PERSON FACTORY

The first Industrial Revolution took place in England and Scotland; the factory was created. The second revolution took place in the United States; the assembly line was created. Change never stops, and the third revolution is about to happen for four reasons: (1) the Internet, (2) 3D design programs, (3) the 3D printer, and (4) nanotechnology.

1. *The Internet.* The Internet enables small producers and subcontractors to get together and make things on their own. If you are making cars, you still need a small factory to assemble the parts, but since we are talking about small-scale production, what is needed is a microfactory. You can design the car of your dreams (perhaps 10 other people share your dream), produce the parts, and go to the microfactory for assembly. It is a tiny market, but it has begun (Local Motors in the United States), and it will grow because we (well, many of us) want our own personal products. Bikes, motorbikes, furniture, and kitchenware can all be made this way. The long value chain with mass production and vertical integration lasted just a hundred years.

2. *The 3D design programs.* With these programs, you can design any product and ask the Internet: "Who can produce these parts, and at what cost?" Small producers

in China or elsewhere can respond, and soon you have your toy helicopter. You can even put a design competition on the Internet; the winner is the best-designed toy helicopter. If a big company does this, it is called crowdsourcing. The question to ask is this: is it likely that your company can get a better design from cyberspace than in-house? If the global Internet market really functions well, then the in-house solution is highly unlikely. There will always be some people from someplace in the world that can do it better. Don't take on the world; join it.

3. *The 3D printer.* In a few years' time, a lot of homes will have one. It is really an inkjet printer without ink, but with plastic or some alloy that can produce products layer by layer. The customers may design their dream product, and the one-person factories will custom-build it. The value chain is not a chain any longer. To sum up: the one-person factory is the greatest innovation in manufacturing since Henry Ford developed the assembly line between 1908 and 1915. The old craftsperson is back. He lost his job to the factories and became a worker; now he is back as a small business owner, this time with new tools to compete with the old workplace.

4. *Nanotechnology.* This is about new materials on a molecular scale. Huge investments in the United States and in the European Union will enable the 3D printer to produce objects made from many different materials.

The era of custom-built products is approaching. We want something personal, and it can be produced more economically with the devices mentioned. A lot of people want to become business owners, and creating things is a dream for many young people. It is a flexible way of entering business; perhaps

you are doing it mostly for fun, but a profit isn't unwelcome. The initial investment is affordable for many people, especially since prices are coming down. In 10 years' time, a 3D printer may cost the same as a TV. The cost of starting a manufacturing company has never been lower.

When we talk about cars (bigger things), you need a real factory; maybe it can be small, but you need one. Many small factories can produce a car (but please buy the engine from a mass-production company). A worldwide net of subcontractors working for themselves is a possibility. Even a village may start producing some custom-built products. It is a dream, but is it a trend? It may become as big as the do-it-yourself market (DIY), and then we will have the revolution. If you have 10,000 3D designs for any product available on the Internet (it is open source), then you have an incentive to buy a 3D printer.

THE AUGMENTED MARKETPLACE

Have you seen a book in which the 3D characters are alive? They act and react based on the information they receive whenever the reader moves. The characters jump, run, and growl. They always look at the camera, giving the impression that they are ready to play and interact with the reader.

They certainly provide a novel reading experience.

They use augmented-reality technologies. In addition to print media, the potential applications in various fields are many.

For years, we have believed that the future is a virtual one, whereas instead it now seems as if augmented reality is where we are headed. Unlike virtual reality, augmented reality does not aim at simulating a reality. It superimposes graphics, audio,

and other sense enhancements onto our daily practices. That is, it enhances our actual perception of reality. For example, when we watch a football game, we see the scores of other games concurrently.

Today only our imagination limits how reality is being augmented. Nowadays, we can ask our computing device where we could stop by to work and use Wi-Fi, and get the information along with user reviews on the atmosphere and the quality of the coffee as well. Or we can ask where the nearest bar is, see how other people have rated it, and in the end ask the way to a taxi. Under other circumstances, if you have trouble finding your car in a large parking lot, an application that points out the right direction and tells the distance to your car might interest you. As wireless computing devices are becoming more widespread and cheaper, new opportunities are emerging to make the user experience of products and services more meaningful.

The revolutionary quality underlying augmented-reality systems is the ability to connect real-time information to a thing or place. This instant information in an appropriate context will change the way people will see and learn from their surroundings. Once they have penetrated the markets, augmented-reality systems will change the way people live, learn, and work in the future.

IF THE QUESTION IS MARKETING, THE ANSWER IS FAN MANAGEMENT

In marketing, new ways of doing things come about gradually, as they should. Today is not like the popular TV series *Mad Men*, but you can easily recognize the way marketing

people worked during the 1960s. There is no revolution waiting around the corner; there is time to adapt. Adapt to what? One change is the personalized ad—from the company to you and you only. The other one is the fan group, the ambassadors, just as in sports.

The direct message to you only is something that some companies are already doing. Amazon is one example. Just like the good salesclerk who knows her customer, Amazon finds out what you have been buying and suggests other books on the same subject. Is this an invasion of privacy? Well, you allow the company to invade and make sure that the offers you receive are relevant ones. Is this the end of mass advertising? Not for the next 10 years, but in the long term.

Fan groups thrive beautifully in sports, and they have been popular for a long time. Now the fan group concept has been introduced to the marketplace thanks to social media. There is one difference, however. The sports fan will support his team irrespective of its results or its quality. The best team will be on the top, but the losing teams have fans, too, fans that stay loyal even when the team keeps losing (OK, there is a limit). As fans, we are not looking for the best product available; we choose with the heart, and we pay to watch our team lose. In the commercial marketplace, however, you buy the best product, not the inferior one; you are not loyal. Perhaps you are when it is about Pepsi versus Coke or about diapers, but those are exceptions. Suppose this product-blind loyalty to sports teams could be moved to your company? Suppose you had a club of loyal fans, customers who were willing to buy the product irrespective of its quality? It would be a nice situation.

The "service" (the sports game) is human; you can identify with the players and you are part of a tribe ("You'll never walk alone," as the song used by the famous Liverpool Football Club

says). It is competitive; your team may lose today, but perhaps it will win next time. Your commercial product is a product; it has no feelings. Perhaps it is a branded product, but its appeal to your heart is weak. Stick to the rules in the marketplace; make sure that yours is the best product, that it has the best quality and the best price. OK, a few companies do have fan clubs (Apple and Virgin Group, for example), but that's because they have CEOs with charisma, and you can't learn charisma. They are the exception to the rule, and they may lose their fan clubs with a new leadership. What you can do is buy into the exciting story, the drama of a sports club; if you do, then some of the loyalty and some of the emotions may be transferred to your company.

Human beings are prepared to die if the story is strong enough. The nation's story, the tribal story, ideology, and the religious story are by far the strongest. You may be willing to fight and die for your country, but not for your company (are we right?). The difference between a sports club and a company is not a real one. Some sports clubs are more commercial than some companies, and the fans know it. Football is competition—some are winning and some are losing. The same thing happens in the marketplace: your company can gain or lose market share—isn't that drama, too? To employees, yes, but normally not to customers. The relative strength of their stories is what makes the real and only difference.

Almost all companies are pretending to act rationally, to suppress emotions. Some have written down "core values," and some do have a program for "corporate social responsibility," but the board may see this as just another way of making money. Does a company have a heart? If the answer is no, then it has no chance of an emotional appeal, a good story, to tell the customers.

Admittedly, a company needs cold blood, but it also needs a warm heart. Why not extend the storytelling to customers? We are seeing more and more value communities. Sports clubs, yes, but we also see movies and books create value communities (remember *Harry Potter*, *Avatar* and *Star Trek*)—again, it can be done if the story is strong enough. The obvious way of creating a value community today is social media, but that is not enough. Most people in your company are not born storytellers, and even fewer CEOs are. But you can ask for help from artistic people. Remember that most customers today do not *need* your product—they buy with their heart. Your story need not be perfect; it just has to be better than the competition's.

Fan management, or the art of creating and managing a group of fans of the company or of your products, is not a possibility; it is a necessity, because this is the future of the marketplace. Modern consumers are more and more critical; they don't trust advertising. They are more segmented, and they are thus more difficult to reach. Use your marketing money to create ambassadors. Customers trust their families, friends, and colleagues. The only way of having this one-on-one relationship is the value community. The Apple story tells it all. Many of us have had this dialogue: somebody asks about your computer brand. Your answer: "I don't remember." You will be told about the beautifully designed Apple products. You are not a creative person unless you have an Apple product. You have met an unpaid ambassador for the company. Did that person believe in the message? Yes, a lot, more than your shop assistant in the IT store.

4

How Will We Learn?

In Chapter 4, we look at the limits of our knowledge, realizing that sometimes people learn more when they are wrong, declaring the end of the isolated mind in learning and in all human action, and taking learning out of the institutions and into daily life. We are almost ready for mind enhancement.

THE LIMITS OF OUR KNOWLEDGE

We know many things, but there is a massive amount of things that we know nothing about. Sure, we have certainly always sensed this, but maybe we have never really explicitly considered it. It may feel somewhat uncomfortable to us.

In addition, the knowledge that we build our futures and base our decisions upon must be only a tiny part of what is knowable. Furthermore, we prefer order over disorder, certainty over uncertainty, and predictability over unpredictability.

Indeed, we have more or less learned to master linearity, but with nonlinearity, science and business are reaching our outer limits.

We might argue that this way of thinking has narrowed our chances of being able to deal with the future.

Our cultural heritage where knowledge is concerned stems from the ancient Greeks. Aristotle set the basis for our understanding of the world. According to him, certain kinds of knowledge (that is, certain kinds of names, terms, ideas, and theories) work best, and sometimes only, within certain areas of expertise and science or certain professions.

For instance, physics is the field of natural movements and transformations, logic is the study of formal reasoning, politics is the analysis of public virtues, and rhetoric is the study of how to convince others.

This is how we comprehend knowledge today. And we have gradually built upon what we know, our body of knowledge has accumulated over the centuries. As a result, human beings have reached an unrivaled position on the planet.

Basically, we believe we should use our knowledge of the past to predict and program the future. In the same way, we should use our knowledge of the past to justify our present and future investments. By doing so, however, we are just pushing the present into the future.

On the other hand, today's science fiction is tomorrow's science.

Certainly today's world is the result of the work of physicists, chemists, and engineers, but it is also the result of the work of moralists, painters, and novelists. There are many people who are adept in various disciplines, but there are few who are capable of imagination. There are fewer still who are capable of subordinating their imagination to systematic planning.

The French philosopher Paul Virilio supposes that as the sphere of what we know has been continuously expanding, the interface with the unknown must also have grown, and will continue to grow out of proportion.

However, the basis on which the future can be known and forged and the traditional strategies for producing knowledge are often bypassed. Instead, we should be seeking novel models, methods, and approaches that are better able to deal with the unknown and uncertainty, not just those that see the future as a continuation of the present.

Furthermore, any organization that follows the trend of giving priority to the present also gives priority to risks and accidents.

Modern civilizations place high value on real time and the short term. Corporations focus on quarter after quarter. They create an extremely thin present.

A thicker present, an extended now, would increase our ability to adapt to changing situations. It would be derived from having a long and rich memory, but also working simultaneously on multiple future time scales. This applies to nations, organizations, and individuals.

With the traditional "scientific" view of looking at the future, decisions about the present are justified based on past knowledge rather than taking into consideration unknown, uncertain, and unpredictable topics.

But we should believe that security in the form of new ideas and innovations comes from the nontraditional, "not scientific" direction.

BEING WRONG

Most of us have always been very careful and tried to avoid mistakes—not just the major, tragic ones, those in traffic or

in hospitals that none of us want to see, but the small errors in everyday life. And we have spent time and energy on eliminating them.

Perhaps we are living a contradiction. By eradicating mistakes, we are giving up the most fertile ground for the novelty and innovation that we claim we crave.

Especially in Western societies, we have been taught to think, or, even better, we have been conditioned to think that order is good. Order is something that must be preserved. If you entertain important guests and you want to make a good impression on them, you will probably clean your table and your room before they arrive. Or if you want to present yourself as a competent manager, you probably try to bring back order as soon as things slip away toward chaos.

In fact, one of the most popular recent business process development ideas is all about avoiding mistakes. "Today's competitive environment leaves no room for error," you can read in a Six Sigma advertisement.

The word *sigma* is a statistical term that measures how far a given process is from perfection. Six Sigma measures how many errors you have in a particular process, so that you can systematically figure out how to eliminate them and get closer to perfection.

Accordingly, companies compete to see who will make the fewest errors. Boards and CEOs can't wait to announce their results to their stakeholders. Consequently, making fewer mistakes is considered synonymous with progress. But it is not progress. It is incremental development, which is all fine and beautiful when the environment is stable.

Hitherto, we have thought that reducing errors is a way to and a sign of success. And we cannot deny that this approach works well in industrial contexts. If your goal is to achieve

something repeatable and predictable, you will be well served by this approach.

With this approach, mistakes are like insects: they are widely despised. In fact, in the information and communications technology community, mistakes are called "bugs." But if you take the insects out of the ecosystem, you will soon notice that you have lost some of the flowers, trees, birds, and bigger animals as well.

We should be on a quest for an alternative theory of progress. The theory that is dominant at present relies on the eradication of mistakes. However, this is counterproductive. It takes a minute to understand that human relationships are too complex to manage according to Six Sigma. Just think of your relationship with your teenage daughter!

Alternatively, any R&D organization that tries to avoid mistakes is also avoiding the interfaces with novelty. On a larger level, communities or nations that believe in and drive toward their own perfection often fail and turn into the opposite of what they dreamed of becoming.

Kathryn Schulz argues that we would be better served by embracing errors and adopting a positive attitude toward them. This means relaxing our need to be right, not considering errors as embarrassing, and ceasing to torment ourselves and others for making mistakes.

We could create environments in which it is safe to fail, promoting tests and pilot projects in schools and organizations instead of using the traditional "stick and carrot" method to reward the correct answers or behavior and to punish mistakes or misbehavior.

There is something contradictory about this. Even if we have been wrong all our lives, there might be something fundamentally constructive in it.

In fact, there are several jobs and situations in which we rarely know in advance what we are looking for. We may have only a vague idea of the direction in which we want to go or what would be an ideal outcome of our effort. Nevertheless, we will eventually get there and get a satisfactory outcome.

Some of us are terrible at following rules and planning our activities in advance. And some of our greatest successes have initially come from mistakes. If we had applied Six Sigma, we would never have achieved them.

CONTAMINATED TRUTH

Let us quote a piece from an excellent book called *Pragmatism*, by William James. It was written more than a century ago, but it still seems to us to be worth studying.

> *Grant an idea to be true. What concrete difference will its being true make to anyone's actual life? What experiences will be different from those which would be obtained if the belief was false? What, in short, is the truth's cash-value in experimental terms?*

This may sound terrifying. Lots of us have always believed that there is a fundamental truth, something solid that we can count on. And we have never thought of what might happen to us if we gave up our ideal of truth.

Most anthropologists agree that ancient people were physically and intellectually as modern as we are today.

Michael Loescher and his coauthors argue that the way they conveyed the knowledge that they acquired and the way in

which knowledge arose for them were the same as they are for us. For thousands of years, we have believed that knowledge arises from three sources:

+ From authority. (You are my boss, so you are probably more right than I am.)
+ From empiricism. (I have seen this work in the past, and I believe it will also work now.)
+ From revelation. (The [spiritual] leader says that this is true.)

In many respects, other than the scientific method, these are still the sources from which our everyday knowledge, beliefs, and conceptions emerge. They are the sources on which we base our evaluations of what is true and what is false. I don't think they have changed, because very little about human beings themselves has changed.

I believe that today we have passed beyond the true and the false, and there is no turning back.

The nature and the distribution of power have changed significantly in recent years. In the past, when we spoke of power, we meant military or political power. Today, power hinges on perceptions. When people's perceptions change, the way they feel, think, and act also changes. As a result, the creation of opportunities and threats depends less on what people have and more on what people think.

Using novel methods to make sense of and imagine the changing world is one thing. Another thing is to manage perceptions—to process new information and incorporate it into a social system for your own purposes, or to reach for emotional control for psychological or political ends.

According to Paul Virilio, in the winter of 2001 the U.S. Department of Defense announced the creation of a new Office of Strategic Influence (OSI) under the control of an assistant secretary of Defense to diffuse false information to influence the hearts and minds of a terrorist enemy. The project, which was designed to manipulate public opinion, was very swiftly canceled.

Perhaps this example is an extreme one. But for some time there have been discussions of whether the Department of Defense should be replaced by the Department of Fear and be run by the movie industry and the mass media. Consequently, the screen and the media have become the battlefields of our times.

Whether it arises from a deliberate attack or from the innocent creation of false impressions as a result of mismatched perceptions, knowledge will become one of the most powerful and frightening forces in a networked world. Together with global media, it will make vast and permanent change possible in short order.

Consequently, perception management has to become a major element in the new intelligence because of threats in the form of influencing public opinion and polluting public emotion.

In my opinion, there is a great risk here. We may gain some short-term benefits by giving up the concept of truth, but in the long term, I believe, we risk the biological and social balance of humanity.

These ideas have been around for a century or more, at least since William James's *Pragmatism*. Two conclusions follow:

1. If we give up the concept of truth, we give up the basis for any reasonable self-reflection.

2. We need to learn and teach our children to become more aware of the information we are dealing with, its origins, and the possible purposes it might serve.

DEEP AQ

Organizations stand and fall by their decision making. The correct decisions have a positive impact on your organization's success; the bad decisions have negative effects.

Increasingly, the competition among organizations depends on how well they can make sense of the data they hold about customers, competitors, and their respective products and services.

In steadier times, decision making was about sensing and responding to changes. Now, given the current uncertainty, predicting and acting play major roles. Accordingly, in a recent Predictive Impact study, 79 percent of large companies announced that they have plans to deploy predictive analysis. It is about having the ability to model and predict behaviors to the point where single decisions are made in real time.

The limits of what is knowable are constantly being pushed forward. For instance, market basket analysis of everyday supermarket purchases produces data that reveal what products are purchased together and what kinds of different baskets are bought by different customers. At call centers, the staff members have information that helps them to offer relevant additional products and services that customers are likely to accept—and feel happy with the service afterward.

The range of data that conclusions are drawn from varies a lot. In addition to the operational databases, call-center notes, e-mails, Internet discussions, and unofficial survey responses are used to improve decision making.

A good way to understand the customer is often to become the customer. For example, if I want to understand Don Quixote, I need to learn Spanish, convert to Catholicism, fight against the Moors or Turks, and forget the history of Europe from 1602 to 2012. Briefly, I need to become Miguel de Cervantes.

Today, data are often further elaborated through automated data preparation and sophisticated, and sometimes interactive, visualizations. As a result, our world is turning into data, turning into calculations, turning into images.

This reminds us of Schrödinger's cat. Once you have figured out where the problem exists, it ceases to exist—or at least solving it becomes possible.

The work can consist of finding little clues to changes in the environment. Likewise, for archaeologists, sometimes a flock of birds or a few horses have led them to the ruins of an amphitheater. Similarly, librarians can reconstitute a lost civilization using the remains of a library.

We must admit that modeling is a frustrating exercise. No model or theory can fully represent the heterogeneity of our world. The famous Austrian philosopher Ludwig Wittgenstein articulated this beautifully. He asked his friend, "Why should I be surprised when you bring me a yellow flower from the field, when I have asked you to bring me a yellow flower?" Certain models bring in certain data. Other models, even based on the same situation, bring in other data.

The limits of our models are the limits of our world. Our language and our models are able to catch only fragments of it. But that is where the danger lurks. Any use of a language, model, or method is a choice, even if it is an arbitrary choice and therefore an act of power. Even though we hold on to the concept of truth, there is always more than one way to describe

a situation, and all of them could be true. Of course, there are some limits in our communication that we cannot cross; if we do, we will lose our credibility. But there is always room for several different presentations of any situation.

In other words, because we cannot scan all the issues all the time, we have to be selective. And we have to try to select the aspects that are most relevant for us, knowing that we will make our decisions based on them.

Even if we were really good and had some extraordinary talent and lots of resources, adapting to changes in the environment remains a great challenge.

I believe that this is why we have created many concepts, such as destiny, luck, and, most recently, serendipity, to fill the gap between our ability to make sense of the world and the actual world.

But without a doubt, human beings can process information and make decisions based on past patterns of success and failure. They can also intentionally pursue changing their systems for their own benefit.

Modeling can assist us in anticipating the future. Many species, not just humans, anticipate because it improves their chances of surviving through evolution. Models guide us in ensuring success and avoiding catastrophe.

Improvements can come from two sources:

1. *The way we perceive our environment.* Of necessity, we have to be selective, because we cannot scan all the things that are happening. We can look at only some aspects of an environment, and hopefully we will learn to select those that are most relevant for us.
2. *The way we perceive our system.* We can perceive our system, not the environment, and learn.

In both cases, memory plays an important role. Every experience leaves a trace in our memory, and we can use that to tune our organization's behavior.

Certainly, modeling is a difficult exercise, but it is not totally hopeless. We are in the beginning phases of developing our understanding of the world. We can expect that, little by little, we will begin to get a fuller, albeit not a perfect, picture of what is going on in our lives.

OUT OF THE INSTITUTIONS

To many people, the single most important element of our society is education. We could even argue that the social significance of schools goes very far. I consider them to be the most beautiful example of social innovation. They stand out as one of the few institutional structures, together with the army and bureaucracy, that has served as an organizational model for centuries.

The schools have safeguarded children while their parents were at work, ensured that they behaved appropriately, and thus ensured that, later in life, they would be able to function within organizations and as citizens.

First, the empirical connection between education and income is clearly positive. A great deal of the difference in income among people is regularly explained by differences in their levels of education.

A U.K. study declares that each additional year of schooling raises earnings by about 10 percent. The OECD Growth Project is slightly more cautious. It says that the long-term economic effect on output of one additional year of education is between 3 and 6 percent.

And what applies to individuals also applies to national economies. There is a statistically significant relationship between the level of human capital and the level of GDP for both the OECD countries and the emerging markets. In the long run, a 10 percent increase in the number of years of education results in an 8 percent increase in per capita GDP in the OECD countries and a 9 percent increase in the emerging markets.

In short, the economic aspect of education is the most vital one. It works in a circular fashion; having a high-level and internationally competitive educational system feeds economic success, and having economic success enables us to sustain or improve our way of life by taking care of children (including educating them), the aged, and those who are less fortunate in life.

Second, we need to focus on the content. Today, jobs for life, state pensions, and paternalistic employers seem to belong to the past. Maybe we need to rethink what should be taught in our schools.

Everybody is guided by some set of assumptions; we could call it a theory about how things work. An appropriate theory organizes the world in a way that leads to positive outcomes; an inappropriate theory can seem to organize the world well, but it will not provide proper solutions. This time we need to get our theory right.

Schooling can no longer be about teaching or about following an agenda that is imposed on people from the top down. Who likes to be told what to do without having any choice in the matter? Do people learn best when they are facing a looming deadline?

In a recent report, even an organization that is clearly part of the establishment, such as the Bureau of European Policy Advisors (BEPA), would prefer to place a greater emphasis on metaskills, such as social skills and adaptability.

That would put the responsibility for learning and achievement in the hands of individuals. Furthermore, it would give room to take into consideration the individual differences among people, allowing them to learn at their own pace and find their own niche, as opposed to one-size-fits-all educational systems.

Increasing our awareness of how the future is built by our present choices and decisions makes us responsible for it. With respect to the present top-down governance, which has demonstrated its limitations over and over again, this approach represents a true alternative: governance driven by informed citizens addressing the global problems from the bottom up.

The Royal Society of Arts, a twenty-first-century enlightenment organization with more than 250 years of tradition, points out that a curriculum that supports emerging, self-organized learning is different from the actual one that exists today. Pupils and students should be able to understand how they learn and how they manage their learning throughout life and to critically access, analyze, and manipulate information.

We should also take into consideration that learning does not happen in a vacuum. Thus, it makes sense to examine how society operates and the impact that different systems, structures, and rules have on the individual. It also makes sense to get familiar with the issues of managing time, risk, and uncertainty and to develop personal strategies for managing change.

Third, do you think that learning will continue to take place within the currently existing institutions? Learning will become as natural as breathing, and our competence will stem from the life we live.

We are moving from heavy enterprise information systems (EIS) to personal information management (PIM). I am constantly stimulating my brain by being around intelligent people

as much as possible, physically and virtually. These connections are my core asset. I believe they will shape me personally and professionally.

Connections are also the core asset for many Internet companies. Today the social graph of connections that Facebook maintains for its 550 million users is perhaps the most valuable asset the company holds. The social graph, the lists of connections, offers a quick and easy way to build networks. No wonder it is seen as a major attractor, engaging people and businesses.

OPEN-SOURCE SCIENCE

You often hear people saying that the software community may offer a more general model for large-scale scientific problem solving, meaning that maybe the point of departure in problem solving should more often be to open up your problem to other people in a systematic way, and to find innovative licensing methods or legal regimes that allow people to share knowledge without risking their overall intellectual property.

We can definitely call our society the "expert society." We have a great belief in and respect for experts. If we are in trouble, one of our favorite problem-solving strategies is to find an appropriate expert and rely on her judgment.

However, a different model has also started to emerge recently. This model rejects the idea of an expert society. Instead, it relies on large and diverse groups of people. It says that there are issues that these groups can answer better than any isolated expert, no matter how intellectually superior he might be in comparison to the members of the groups.

At the same time, we are seeing a growing use of collaborative methods. They make use of the cumulative wisdom of the scientific analysis of dozens, hundreds, or sometimes thousands of participants. The people using these methods claim that although the observations made by a single person may not be individually insightful, the accumulated, and occasionally averaged, efforts can be dazzling.

You could, for instance, repeat the experiment that Thomas C. Schelling did in New York. He asked his students, where would you go in order to be most likely to meet someone? And at what time? A majority of the students named the same meeting place: the information booth at Grand Central Station. And almost all of them would go there at noon. Where would the people in your city meet, and at what time?

Another line concerning collaborative thinking looks for analogies and metaphors from nature to help us to understand our own behavior. For example, the flocking of starlings can be explained with three simple rules: (1) stay as close to the middle as possible, (2) stay two body lengths away from your neighbors, and (3) do not bump into another starling. Each starling is acting on its own. Nevertheless, a kind of organized, bottom-up behavior is achieved, giving the individual birds protection and a better chance of surviving. The example is then applied to make sense of grocery stores, financial markets, and politics.

I think we should pay attention to how and when this approach works. Otherwise, this "wisdom of crowds" turns into "stupidity of crowds."

According to Martha Lagace's article on HBS Working Knowledge, an open-source community could serve more widely as an organizing model in our societies, especially in three specific cases:

1. *Mass analysis*, in which a large number of people take a look at a set of data in order to find mistakes or hidden details. The ability of groups to act collectively to analyze and generate information is one of the drivers of collaborative efforts in Wikipedia; no individual contributor would be able to create such a large and reliable body of knowledge in his lifetime, but with a mass of authors, the work was done in a relatively short time.

2. *Mass evaluation*, in which a large number of people are given the opportunity to vet researchers' articles and arguments. This is a more qualitative and subjective approach than mass analysis, but it can produce good results. An example is *arXiv*, the physics preprint journal, which allows anyone to contribute articles and lets participants evaluate them.

3. *Collaborative research*, where research that is already in progress is opened up to allow laboratories anywhere in the world to contribute to it. The networked nature of modern science and the brief downtime between projects make the concept quite feasible, and it spreads new ideas and discoveries faster, accelerating scientific process globally.

The outcomes being pursued are still in accordance with the best traditions of science (critical engagement, open discourse, and cooperation), but the methods for achieving these goals are of the twenty-first century.

On the other hand, an extremely insightful intelligence report, *Proteus*, gives three basic reasons why we should be careful not to apply the open-source model without carefully considering when and how to do it:

1. In an interconnected world of global networks, the speed with which new knowledge is created is nothing short of remarkable.
2. The new knowledge is silent as to its intrinsic truth or falsehood.
3. In a world of instant networks, what is false can become true, and what is true can become false; the concept of ground truth is dangerously limiting.

Can we build our future on this kind of knowledge? Can we even call it knowledge? It is opinion. But definitely, we should study the opportunity in more detail.

THE NEW NOMADS

Sometimes, when you sit in a train, the people around you are looking at their cell phones; occasionally they put them to their ear. They seem to have a life someplace else—the train does not matter at all. Even if you are sitting with friends, you are in contact with somebody who is not on the train.

We remember that people had a life even before the cell phone. In those days, social contacts needed geography; you got together physically. Not anymore. The new nomads—the new lives—are coming.

In 10 years, we will all have an e-bag, our own electronic companion that is vital for our life and is more important than your purse or your car keys. This is because everything is in your e-bag, and if you lose it, you are lost; you become a non-person. You can work from it, you can pay your bills and buy things from it, and you can use it to watch films and read and watch news and magazines. You can get all the information

in the world and then some. Your friends and family are only one click away. It is your guide to everything, including your health. It is your identity. It is you.

It is called an e-bag because you need a bag for it—a bag with a nice personal design. Today we have several devices: the laptop, the cell phone, the TV, and the tablet. They will merge into one device (all in one), and the cell phone will be able to do most of what the laptop does today.

Where are our customers? They are in the e-bag; that's where you can reach them with ads, with information about upcoming events, and with bills. Your geographical address (where you live) doesn't matter. The tax people will contact you at your e-bag, not your home.

The new nomads will be in contact with anybody, anytime, anywhere—and in colors or even 3D. Is this a life? What about having a beer with your friends? You will still be able to do that, but the amount of time you are in virtual contact with somebody will increase a lot and the amount of time you sit with people and talk and drink will decrease. The number of friends you have will be much higher, but your contacts with them will be shorter and more superficial. The number of deep friendships you have—those people whom you trust and with whom you can talk about any subject—will go down. Trust is built when you do sit down and talk—when you get to know the other person, when body language is added to the words. Trust may go down. Can you become lonely if all your contacts come through your e-bag? Sure, but you will still have a home and a family.

Or do we still need a home? For love, for children, for sleeping, eating, and personal care, we still need it. But it will be a rest station, with fewer activities unless we choose to engage in them. When we get married at around 30 years of age (as most

people do), the nest building will start, but not much before. For younger people, the home may function more like a hotel.

Twenty-five years ago, we had two important pillars: the home and the workplace. Today, a lot of work can be done away from the office, and a lot of the activities that are done in the home could take place somewhere else. Some cafés around the world are trying to introduce themselves as "the third place" (away from home and the workplace), and they have already had some success.

The good old reception-style interaction may fit these new nomads perfectly. Suppose there is a café with no chairs, where people move around and talk. There's no need to be with the same people at a certain table all the time. You need to become a member of the club, and "introducers" may facilitate casual meetings.

The "office hotel" of today offers an address and a desk plus access to the world for certain small companies that are on the move—they can claim some semblance of permanency. There's no need to invest in a permanent office. Likewise, a "home hotel" may suit the new nomads. There will be no need to invest in furniture and rent for a long period. The hotel will do the cleaning, of course. The traditional concept of the hotel (a place for people who are away from home) may change, or rather be supplemented by this new concept.

E-bag theft and identity fraud will be a growing problem in a globalized world, but on the other hand, authorities will always be able to locate the e-bag, and therefore they will be able to find either you or the thief: it will have a GPS built into it.

Not all of us will become "new nomads." The traditional family, with its heirlooms and common dinners prepared in the kitchen, will still exist, but it will become a segment or at least become less mainstream than it is now.

THE END OF THE ISOLATED MIND

For Plato, love is an intermediate stage between possessing and not possessing. It is in the inner subjective life of a person. For a person who is always striving, never satisfied, but always becoming, love is the true condition.

However, in Western philosophy, the myth of the isolated mind has governed our learning and teaching practices for centuries. From the Cartesian perspective, the mind of a human being is seen as an essentially self-closed entity. The human mind has an inside, and it causally interacts with things outside of it. In other words, the external world and the mind are two separate entities.

Each and every one of us is born undifferentiated from the world, and we are born with basic biological needs that require constant or periodic satisfaction. To satisfy these needs, we become caught up in the dialectics of exchanges with others.

Beginning in the early stages of our lives, some objects can become desirable because others desire them. A teenager's argument that she needs something "because everybody else has it" is familiar to every parent. And when others' desire is withdrawn, the objects lose their allure. A hungry child might refuse to eat if she senses that the food is not offered with love and affection.

Our desires and decisions both affect and are affected by the desires and decisions of others. How we end up depends on our ability to play the game of life.

The French philosopher Jacques Lacan talks about how we depend on the existence of "the other" to fill the gap in our desires. He does not mean only the triviality that humans desire others sexually. He means a more general demand for the recognition and love of other people. He even goes beyond

human interactions and argues that everyday events, such as listening to music, tasting food, or taking a shower, also link us to our environment and influence our existence.

He rejects Cartesian thinking, and his good advice is that we should be very careful with approaches, both to learning and more generally, that are clearly based on it.

Human beings are embedded in intersubjective systems. In any social encounter, the way a situation develops depends both on us and on other people and their opinions. We do not come to these encounters totally open; we have some baggage (our histories and our ideas about our futures), and others also have theirs.

This basically means that learning can occur in two ways:

1. When we alter our mindsets, mental models, or basic ideas about our work or our future
2. When we meet and interact with one another, and thus expand our subjective worlds

We can go further and suggest that the quality of the emotional feedback, both positive and negative, that we get from our fellow human beings significantly shapes our lives.

Negative emotions are more powerful and more attention grabbing than positive ones. They are critical to survival, because they narrow a person's thought-action repertoires and thus enable him to take the decisive actions needed to deal with threatening situations.

In everyday life, negative feedback makes us more cautious and limits our range of action.

Barbara Fredricsson celebrates positive emotions such as love, joy, interest, gratitude, and enthusiasm because they broaden our momentary thought-action repertoires. They fuel

our future success. They are the means of creating an upward spiral in an organization, city, or nation that will build emotional and intellectual resources for the future.

MIND ENHANCEMENT

According to *Nature* magazine, 7 percent of students in U.S. universities overall and up to 25 percent of students on some campuses have used prescription drugs to get higher grades or to increase their capacity for learning in some measurable way in the past year.

We might presume that they are only the early adopters, and that the trend is going to grow. There is also an argument that calls for public policies to help societies accept the benefits of cognitive enhancement.

Some people say that we should welcome new methods of improving our brains. The brain is a physical organ, just like the heart or the lungs. Its functioning can be enhanced, particularly by the substances we put in our bodies. Today people live and work much longer than they used to. Also, pharmacological enhancement tools are necessary to improve the quality of life and to increase work productivity.

This argument is once again relying on a mechanistic view of human nature, looking to enhance students' minds by increasing their capacity to store more information and to process it faster. This is a very reductionist take on human beings.

At the moment, doing this is illegal. The transactions described are considered crimes, and they are punishable by prison. Nevertheless, we should not forget that rules and laws are conventional; sometimes they can and should be changed.

Most of our lives, at home and at work, bear little relation to the natural state of our species. We wear clothes, prepare our meals, and live in highly sophisticated buildings. To put it briefly, we have shaped our environments significantly.

There are two approaches to mind enhancement.

The first one involves cognition-enhancing drugs, or nootropics, if you prefer. This is still a controversial issue.

On the one hand, there are those who are unsure about whether drugs that can enhance cognition beyond normal levels in healthy people really exist. They admit that there have been positive results with cognition-enhancing drugs, but they call for more research.

On the other hand, there are several prominent researchers who are convinced that there is room for responsible use of these drugs. They place cognition-enhancing drugs in the same category as exercise, nutrition, and sleep, and consider them morally equivalent to those more traditional enhancements.

The second approach concerns mind-enhancing machines, or new and better ways to process information. They might involve skills like leadership, communication, learning, problem solving, decision making, time management, and stress management. More generally, though, they are instruments empowered by human beings that transform the effort into results that cannot be replicated without the instrument, or that can be obtained without it only at a much slower pace and at the cost of painstaking work. The abacus, writing, and visual modeling fall into this category.

Contemporary mind-enhancing machines exploit the phase differences among the senses and model experiments that draw on several senses jointly. Associations between senses are preferred—for instance, touch with figures, sound with text, and vision with contents. The target is to capitalize on the joint

capacity of the human senses to integrate information through various channels. It is like when we ate at Dinner by Heston in London and enjoyed a multisensory experience.

We are natural-born cyborgs, and the Internet is our giant extended mind.

For centuries, scientists have been focused on the brain. Long ago, it was seen as a machine. In the last century, it was common to speak about the brain as a kind of computer. Most recently, the Swiss army knife metaphor has appeared. It seems to fit with what we have learned about the brain: the visual cortex processes what we see, Broca's area is the center for language, and other areas deal with other specific functions.

As we learn more, it is clear that the brain's work depends on how well the different parts are linked together. For me, the brain looks more like the Internet. The interconnected neural networks are distributed intelligence that closely matches the World Wide Web.

While our mind is holding and processing a huge amount of information, the neurons are continuously being reorganized, and new feedback loops are established.

When we woke up this morning, we were a new person—literally.

Our mind moves smoothly between outside and inside sources, showing no interest in where its information comes from. In fact, humans are proving to be good at merging mind and machine.

From an evolutionary perspective, there is nothing unnatural about relying on the Internet for information. After all, the survival of our species has always depended on our ability to constantly consult and adapt to the world around us. The new technologies are just the current state of the development.

The rate of technological change has been constantly accelerating. If it continues the way it has been going, within a quarter of a century, the intelligence of machines will exceed that of humans. The machines will have emotions and a wide range of skills, including those demanding abstract and creative thinking and physical movement. In 10 years, a $1,000 computer will match the processing power of the human brain. In 20 years, the same computer will equal 1,000 brains.

Recently, Ken Jennings, who is famous for his 74 victories in a row on the television quiz show *Jeopardy*, had to admit his defeat by an IBM computer. Watson, as the computer is called, is a question-answering machine that can understand and answer questions posed in natural language.

Although it defeated its human opponents, Watson proved to be imperfect. However, it was capable of dealing with issues that were previously considered impossible for artificial intelligence: untangling convoluted and opaque statements and making and evaluating quick and simultaneously strategic choices.

In front of us, we can see an era in which the lives of human beings will be both enriched and challenged. There will be a union between humans and machines, and as a result our brains will be equipped with greater capacity, speed, and knowledge-sharing ability.

This merging will enable us to transcend our biological limitations. There will no longer be clear distinctions between humans and machines or between real reality and virtual reality. Our intelligence will become increasingly nonbiological.

The practical consequences follow. We will be better positioned to tackle some of the "eternal challenges," such as aging and illness, hunger and poverty. And if we remain human and have our heart in the right place, we can also tackle greater challenges concerning the future of our planet.

5

Thinking About Systems

This chapter provides the reader with the big picture. It looks at our planet as a system of systems in which everything affects everything else, evaluates how human activities affect the planet, talks about the big society and new economics, and in the end discovers new marketplaces.

A SYSTEM OF SYSTEMS

Don't you sometimes get tired of watching all these news channels? In some hotel lobbies, they are showing BBC News around the clock; in others, they run CNN.

And why the continuous communication about crisis after crisis? Why must a piece of news be something horrible—a personal meltdown, crime, or murder—before it makes its way to the television? Or a tsunami, war, or financial crisis?

Certainly only exceptional events make it to the news, and it's easier for bad news than for good news. And the way we

have handled the Iraq War, the financial crisis, and the recession that followed it have certainly uncovered not only how much we depend on one another, but also major shortcomings in how we respond to others.

You have probably heard about system of systems from many mouths. International organizations, military strategists, and large multinational corporations have had the term in their vocabulary for three decades.

Yet it has finally reached the mainstream thinking. There are perhaps two reasons for this:

1. Rather than talking about an isolated financial crisis, we have come to see that it was not a one-off event. The financial crisis has also raised our awareness of the level of interconnectedness in the world and made clear our current incapability to make sense of and manage systemic risks collectively.

2. Beyond the two billion people connected through the Internet, we are also connected by trillions of smart objects. In brief, already existing technology— embedded sensors, increased computing power, and sophisticated algorithms—is enabling us to apply the system of systems approach.

Nevertheless, we are still trapped by the current short-term pressures facing individuals, companies, and governments. In addition, everyone has his own responsibilities and therefore optimizes accordingly.

We can draw a figure of the global system of systems. According to the IBM Global Business Report, it would consist of 11 core systems that have evolved over time to serve specific

needs in societies. All together, these 11 systems represent 100 percent of the world's GDP.

To call these systems interrelated is an understatement. They are highly dependent on one another. In each system, there are public and private organizations that span multiple industries and every level from city councils to international transport authorities. As a result of these complex relationships and transactions among the actors, a specific need will be fulfilled. Out of the 11 systems, the biggest in absolute numbers are infrastructure, leisure, and transportation.

If we observe, for instance, the transportation system carefully, we find out (the biggest ball within the transportation ball) that it involves a number of players from the same industry, such as automobile, railway, travel, and aerospace organizations. The smaller balls indicate the related players: trade partners, material providers, energy resources, logistics, and other service supporters. The size of each ball represents each system's economic value. On average, other systems contribute about half of each system's input.

We can analyze all the systems in a similar way, remembering that the arrows in the figure represent the strength of the interactions between the systems. The bolder the arrow, the more powerful, economically, the relationship is.

We call for a new mindset, as represented in Table 5.1.

TABLE 5.1   Systemic Mindset

From	To
Siloed approach	System of systems approach
Suboptimization	System-level optimization
Short-term focus	Long-term focus

This change in thinking is supported by changes in values, attitudes, and perspectives. We can discuss and argue over problems and solutions from a holistic point of view to make better sense of global systemic risks, and maybe, if we take the responsibility for today's decisions and their meaning for tomorrow, build a more sustainable planet. It seems that the ideas for a fundamental change are there.

THE PLANES OF INFLUENCE

We all must have had the feeling, "I must know some of the movie stars better than I know my actual neighbors." We know the names of Angelina Jolie and Brad Pitt's children, but not those playing in our backyard.

Thanks to global media, geographical distances have been reduced to zero. You can hear the news concerning your favorite celebrities instantly, be aware of discoveries that happen in physics and chemistry, or be informed about political decisions and natural disasters that take place anywhere in the world.

Things have turned around. Those nearest to you are strangers, and the exotic are neighbors. The local has become the exterior, and the global the interior. Our world is redefined by instantaneous information and communication. Real-time exchanges of information win over real-space exchanges.

We could talk about planes of influence. To me, they represent those places where we can influence others, and others can influence us. Certainly, you have been influenced by global media.

According to Michael Loescher et al., today and tomorrow, the planes of influence are:

+ *Terrestrial.* The geopolitical domains of air, sea, undersea, and land, as well as the physical concentrations of wealth (for example, sea lanes and oil fields).
+ *Space.* The world of satellites and future space platforms.
+ *Spectral.* The electromagnetic spectrum, in which so much of the electronic warfare, frequency management, and sensing occurs today.
+ *Virtual.* The global world of networks and connectivity.
+ *Psychological.* Those media and conduits that can be used to influence the hearts and minds of people.

Surely we can communicate and cooperate with one another if we live in the same building or in the same town.

But we can also do so if we share the same level of influence. Thus, watching television, listening to the radio, and diving into the Internet are enough to enable us to get influences from beyond our physical world. And those influences are just as real and meaningful to us as those physical ones are.

On a larger scale, the history of our species to date has been about conquering lands and seas (the physical spaces of the planet), but recently it is coming to be more about creating new realities to command and control, that is, on the space, spectral, virtual, and emotional planes.

Thus, the ability to orchestrate events across the different venues, either in sequence or in parallel, to influence opinion and to create meaning is of strategic importance. In other words, time is often the analytical nexus behind seemingly disparate events.

The timing of press releases, diplomatic actions, or corporate mergers largely dictates their success or failure. On the

other hand, we can see the inklings of this ability in our personal lives. Global media penetrate into local realities and fill them with the news of newborn celebrity babies, royal weddings, and all kinds of important events.

Innovation is expensive, takes time, and is difficult to achieve. We are tempted to try other kinds of strategies. We should copy with pride. However, we should not copy just anyone. We should be aware of which people or products are worth copying; we should have real-time knowledge about what is going on in the world, because innovation has a time and a place.

When the first iPhone came on the market, it took six days to reproduce it in China. Any haute couture you see on the catwalk in Paris (pick your favorite Dior, Chanel, or Hermès) can and will be copied by Chinese entrepreneurs within two days.

Socially, the speed of light at which global mass media synchronize opinions and decisions worries me. It shatters the plurality of social times.

Our daily, weekly, and monthly routines remain specific. The beginning and end of the school days, working days, and holidays vary from nation to nation. The opening and closing times in the factories and the fiscal and budgetary cycles are different in different nations, regions, and organizations. And so are municipal and national elections and other political activities.

These routines construct our everyday lives and produce socially important knowledge. However, and herein lies the danger, globally networked immediacy may affect the long durations of familial relations and the conditions of local and regional economies.

PLANETARY BOUNDARIES

Maybe we need to try to comprehend not only human and business activities, but the complex interdependencies between the planet's natural systems and human activities.

But do we dare to do so? After all, we are children of the Newtonian paradigm. Since its formulation, it has been extremely successful, and it has been applied in areas that are far beyond its original purpose. But Newtonian systems are closed systems; they don't look at what happens outside the machine or the factory or at what the overall consequences of their function are. Neither do they allow anything from outside them or our desires to influence them.

For 10,000 years, our planet's environment has been unusually stable. The geologists call this era the Holocene. Today, that stability is under threat. Since the beginning of the industrial age, a new era has arisen, one in which human actions have become the main driver of global environmental change. Human activities are pushing the earth away from the stable Holocene state, with detrimental consequences for large parts of the world.

We can briefly demonstrate the actual situation.

The world average figure means that in 2012, the earth's available resources for the year were consumed by August 22.

If everybody on the planet lived and consumed the way the Americans do, we would actually need four more globes the size of ours to provide the necessary resources for that. If instead everybody lived like the British, the number of additional globes needed would be 2½.

At the moment, the Chinese have their consumption balanced with the earth's resources, and the Indians would need

only 40 percent of the world's resources to maintain their way of life. Although I do not like to make extrapolations, it is obvious that if China and India want to have and in fact achieve the same standard of living as the United States and the United Kingdom, the stress on the planet will increase enormously.

This issue divides people. There are those who are minimally committed and delay every concrete action, and there are those who believe that we are moving too slowly and taking too tiny steps.

We need a rigorous methodology. We need to undertake expert solicitation and deep literature reviews in order to describe the base conditions for global sustainability.

We need clear thinking. The nine planetary boundaries given here, developed by Johan Rockström, indicate the limits of the earth's ability to support human civilization. They can be measured across several natural systems.

- *The stratospheric ozone layer.* This filters out ultraviolet radiation from the sun. If this layer decreases, increasing amounts of ultraviolet (UV) radiation will reach ground level. This can cause a higher incidence of skin cancer in humans, and also damage terrestrial and marine biological systems.
- *Biodiversity.* In the Millennium Ecosystem Assessment of 2005, it was concluded that changes in biodiversity as a result of human activities have been more rapid in the past 50 years than at any other time in human history, and that the drivers of change that cause biodiversity loss and lead to changes in ecosystem services either are steady, show no evidence of declining over time, or are increasing in intensity.

- *Chemical dispersion.* Emissions of persistent toxic compounds, such as metals, various organic compounds, and radionuclides, are some of the key human-driven changes to the planetary environment. There are a number of examples of additive and synergistic effects from these compounds. These effects are potentially irreversible. Those that are of most concern are reduced fertility and especially the potential for permanent genetic damage.

- *Climate change.* We have reached a point where the loss of summer polar ice is almost certainly irreversible. From the perspective of the earth as a complex system, this is one example of a sharp threshold, above which large feedback mechanisms could drive the earth system into a much warmer, greenhouse gas–rich state, with sea levels meters higher than at present. Recent evidence suggests that the earth system, which is now passing 387 parts per million by volume (ppmv) of CO_2, has already transgressed this planetary boundary.

- *Ocean acidification.* About a quarter of the CO_2 that humanity produces is dissolved in the oceans. Here it forms carbonic acid, altering ocean chemistry and decreasing the pH of the surface water. Increased acidity reduces the amount of available carbonate ions, an essential building block for shell and skeleton formation in organisms such as corals and some shellfish and plankton species. This will seriously change the ocean ecology and potentially lead to drastic reductions in fish stocks. Compared to preindustrial times, surface ocean acidity has increased by 30 percent.

- *Freshwater consumption and the global hydrologic cycle.* The freshwater cycle is both a major prerequisite for

staying within the climate boundary and is strongly affected by climate change. Human demand is now the dominating driving force determining the function and distribution of global freshwater systems. The effects are dramatic, including both global-scale changes in river flow and shifts in vapor flows from changes in land use.

* *Land system change.* Land is being converted for human use all over the planet. Forests, wetlands, and other such areas are being converted primarily to agricultural land. This change in land use is one of the driving forces behind reduced biodiversity, and it also has impacts on water flows and on carbon and other cycles.

* *Nitrogen and phosphorus inputs into the biosphere and the oceans.* Human modification of the nitrogen cycle has been even greater than our modification of the carbon cycle. Human activities now convert more N_2 from the atmosphere into reactive forms than all of the earth's terrestrial processes combined. Much of this new reactive nitrogen pollutes waterways and coastal zones, is emitted into the atmosphere in various forms, or accumulates in the terrestrial biosphere.

* *Atmospheric aerosol loading.* This is considered a planetary boundary for two main reasons: (1) the influence of aerosols on the climate system, and (2) their adverse effects on human health on a regional and global scale. Without aerosol particles in the atmosphere, we would not have clouds. Most clouds and aerosol particles act to cool the planet by reflecting incoming sunlight back to space. However, some particles (such as soot) and thin high clouds act like greenhouse gases to warm the planet. In addition, aerosols have been shown to affect monsoon circulations and global-scale circulation systems.

To be exact, we have already transgressed three of these boundaries: climate change, rate of biodiversity loss, and interference with the nitrogen cycle.

The evidence for our having crossed the first boundary is the increased concentration of carbon dioxide in the atmosphere. For the latter two boundaries, we can verify the change by measuring the rate of species loss and the rate at which N_2 is removed from the atmosphere and converted to reactive nitrogen.

In addition, we are approaching the boundaries for freshwater use, changes in land use, ocean acidification, and interference with the global phosphorus cycle.

Our industrial systems are built on carbon-based energy and unsustainable resource demands. They are endangering our societies and our planet.

Raising people's awareness and reforming our policies are necessary. Ultimately, though, we need to create a postcarbon economy and turn our industries into a force for sustainable wealth generation. This is the biggest challenge of our lifetime.

NEW ECONOMICS

There is no denying it; we are all aware of the financial crisis. Something does not work. We have noticed that there is a problem, recognized a bunch of subproblems, and finally started to fix it. That is our modus operandi. However, what if there is something more to it? Then our approach will not work.

One of the most influential phrases that has shaped and describes the moral set of financial markets was written in the eighteenth century by philosopher Bernard Mandeville. He

wrote, "Private Vices by the dextrous management of a skilful Politician may be turned into Publick Benefits."

The lesson he taught was that individuals and individual organizations can be greedy because the cumulative effect of their selfish actions would maximize the collective benefit. Many people persist in holding this belief, and it is conveniently and repeatedly used to justify numerous choices and decisions.

It is assumed that markets are in equilibrium. When informed actors pursue their own goals and trade among themselves, demand and supply will eventually balance, and the resulting prices will provide the best possible estimates of value.

It is also assumed that small causes have small effects and big causes have big effects. This is called linear causality. It is the logic that is embedded in the models and tools used in financial markets.

The excellent Oxford scenarios look beyond the financial crisis and briefly summarize nine fundamental ideas that are driving mainstream economics:

1. What you cannot count does not count.
2. The environment is an externality; it does not count.
3. What cannot be measured cannot be managed.
4. Forgoing near-term profits for long-term benefits is irrational.
5. Probability and risk can be priced.
6. Everything else also has its price.
7. Profit maximization equals social responsibility.
8. Markets are efficient and regulation inefficient.
9. The past can be used to model and predict the future.

For us, that is toxic thinking. The consequences can be seen in the financial crisis and the recession that followed.

But that's not the worst thing. If the situation weren't so serious, we would call it hilarious. The worst thing is that the failure that occurred is considered a failure of control, supervision, and regulation. Concomitantly, the remedy is that we need to improve them and create even more of them.

That is like pushing the toothpaste back into the tube.

As a result of the crisis, middle-class people have lost the savings that they worked hard for all their lives, and the poor are once again pushed to their limits and further just to survive.

The mainstream economic theory is more like an objective science such as physics or mathematics than like a human or moral science.

The limitations of the theory had already been discussed frequently before the current financial crisis, but the dissenting voices have usually been ignored. On at least two occasions, however, they could not be silenced.

First, when complex derivatives and packages of derivatives initially became popular among economists, there was no reliable way of assessing their value. Then, in 1973, Robert Merton presented a model based on the Black-Scholes equation that served the economists' needs. Later it became the standard formula for making the value of options objective. Simultaneously, there was an enormous increase in the volume of derivatives.

To put it simply, the model requires a set of key inputs by the user, especially an estimate of market volatility. Naturally, when the market dynamics change, the value of the options changes.

In 1998, the hedge fund Long-Term Capital Management (LTCM) collapsed. Notably, it had both Merton and Scholes on its board. LTCM had more than a trillion dollars in positions, and these had to be unwound, leading to losses of

$4.6 billion. The company was playing a likely probability of a small gain against a small probability of a very large loss. Consequently, a Federal Reserve bailout and government intervention were required to stabilize the financial markets.

Second, let's take a very different example. In 2000, French university students protested against an exclusive focus on mainstream textbooks and mathematical methods. The protest was noticed and also supported internationally.

In other words, despite the warning example of the LTCM collapse, and despite criticism of the widespread adoption of the tools and material that were used in teaching, a system-level catastrophe was just waiting to happen.

Therefore, a new point of departure must be defined.

The basic assumptions of mainstream economics—rational actors and market equilibrium—are demonstrably unfounded in the real world. Furthermore, I claim that they preclude in principle an understanding of nonlinear and disruptive events, such as the financial crisis.

The socioeconomic system is so complex and nondeterministic that no formal modeling or outsourcing of the human intelligence to models and tools can explain everything or be capable of precise prediction.

Naturally, these views challenge the existing assumptions. However, if they were accepted as the foundation for a new theory of economics, it would certainly look different from the present one. It would include:

1. A revised understanding of the underpinnings of the socioeconomic system
2. A theoretically and methodologically more diverse approach and a good contextual understanding of which theories and tools are appropriate to use

3. A wider scope of economics education, encompassing different opinions

The question is: Do we have the courage to change the thinking behind our economic systems? And can we change the practices to be in accord with this? Or do we really have a choice? How much time do we have to make the change? When is it probable that the current system will fail again?

SMALL STATE, BIG SOCIETY

In most parts of the world, the states have been grabbing ever-larger shares of the economies for almost a century. Naturally, we are now referring to industrialized countries such as Austria, Belgium, Britain, Canada, France, Germany, Italy, Japan, the Netherlands, Spain, Sweden, Switzerland, the United States, and many countries like them.

Two things seem to go together: governments that have been expanding, and people who have been fretting about it.

In 1888, the French economist Pierre Paul Leroy calculated that 12 to 13 percent of GDP was a sustainable limit for a modern state. Nevertheless, by 1960, the welfare states had pushed the average to 28 percent. In the meantime, the world-famous economist Friedrich Hayek stated that government regulation might destroy the forces that have made advances possible. In the 1990s, President Bill Clinton and other Western leaders declared the end of big government. And look what happened. In the United Kingdom, under New Labour, the state's share rose from 37 percent in 2000 to 44 percent in 2007. And at the same time, in the United States, the Republican government pushed up spending more than any government in 40 years.

Table 5.2 reveals data from the *Economist* showing the overall growth in government over the last hundred years.

TABLE 5.2 Government Spending as an Average Percentage of GDP

	1870	1913	1920	1937	1960	1980	1990	2000	2009
Austria	10.5	17.0	14.7	20.6	35.7	48.1	38.6	52.1	52.3
Belgium	NA	13.8	22.1	21.8	30.3	58.6	54.8	49.1	54.0
Britain	9.4	12.7	26.2	30.0	32.2	43.0	39.9	36.6	47.2
Canada	NA	NA	16.7	25.0	28.6	38.8	46.0	40.6	43.8
France	12.6	17.0	27.6	29.0	34.6	46.1	49.8	51.6	56.0
Germany	10.0	14.8	25.0	34.1	32.4	47.9	45.1	45.1	47.6
Holland	9.1	9.0	13.5	19.0	33.7	55.8	54.1	44.2	50.0
Italy	13.7	17.1	30.1	31.1	30.1	42.1	53.4	46.2	51.9
Japan	8.8	8.3	14.8	25.4	17.5	32.0	31.3	37.3	39.7
Spain	NA	11.0	8.3	13.2	18.8	32.2	42.0	39.1	45.8
Sweden	5.7	10.4	10.9	16.5	31.0	60.1	59.1	52.7	52.7
Switzerland	16.5	14.0	17.0	24.1	17.2	32.8	33.5	33.7	36.7
United States	7.3	7.5	12.1	19.7	27.0	31.4	33.3	32.8	42.2
AVERAGE	10.4	12.7	18.4	23.8	28.4	43.8	44.7	43.2	47.7

A diet is necessary. There are two obvious recipes for it: (1) to learn how to do more with less, which would mean reengineering the state, or (2) to learn how to live with less, which would mean giving up a number of currently available social benefits.

For China and India, the problem is the opposite. Just as human beings have two legs, China and India have a long

economic leg and a very short social one. They would walk better if their legs were of equal length.

Once again, new ideas about the state seem to be coming from England.

But first, to really understand where we are coming from and possibly going to, I can briefly explain recent history. In the nineteenth century, the British were the liberals who championed modernization and campaigned for free trade. They prided themselves on their lean government in India: just a few thousand bureaucrats.

By the turn of the twentieth century, "New Liberals" had started to question the morality of the night-watchman state. What kind of liberty was there if so many men and women still lived in misery and ignorance? A bigger and more active state became the answer. In came compulsory education, laws and regulations to take care of the people, and more taxes to fund welfare and public libraries.

England, followed by and accompanied with several other countries, continued on its chosen road for most of the twentieth century, until the first critics began to emerge. Now I see that there is a new radicalism in the air. The state may be changing course again. This course might involve reducing the size of the state and building a postbureaucratic state. Yes, that's the same term that Tony Blair used when he was prime minister.

The circling ideas are coming together under three buzzwords: pluralism, localism, and voluntarism.

We cannot expect the diet to be easy. There are numerous vested interests involved.

The growth of the public sector has been encouraged by political parties and unions from both the left and the right, by civil servants who are keen on keeping their jobs, and by companies that work closely with and depend on public-sector funding.

I am afraid that for many countries, just maintaining the actual weight, or keeping the state at its present size, will take hard work.

This time, however, there are several external factors that must be taken into consideration. The first one is the enormous economic pressure that comes from the deficits. In the debate over how to deal with that, the sizes and the spending of governments are hot topics in the United States, the United Kingdom, and the European Union more generally. The second reason is globalization. The mobility of people, businesses, and capital limits governments' ability to keep on raising taxes. The third reason is the growing body of evidence showing that states that are too big get in the way of social progress. When a state takes more than half of the GDP, the benefits become harder to demonstrate and the costs harder to hide.

The debate is very much about two relationships: that between public and private, and that between government and the citizens. More precisely, the debate is very much about renegotiating the two relationships: rejecting the traditional master-servant relationship and establishing a more balanced one.

In addition to top-down governance, this is about exploring the business-led and citizen-led possibilities. The objective is not only to have companies become more actively involved in local life and policy, but also to get people to engage with one another for their own and the community's good.

That means changing from a big state to a big society.

ECONOMICS OF BITS

Have you noticed that the devices that we need in order to do our work are mostly free? All right, as of now, nobody is giving

us free computers, but we run them with a free Linux operating system, and we use free Google Docs.

And that's without mentioning everything else that we do, from e-mails to Twitter. When selecting hotels, restaurants, and cafes, we make our choices based on whether or not they have free wireless access. And naturally we Skype our phone calls.

Free services have entered our lives gradually. Service by service, we have accepted them and applied them in our essential everyday practices.

If we study the structures of industrial revolutions carefully, we find that they have one thing in common: at least one key factor of production is drastically reduced in cost.

During evolutionary periods, there is lots of excitement. Many weak signals and bubbles are stillborn, as none of them can lead to a revolution until the whole platform—that is to say, the main drivers of the development, which always require a long time period—is ready.

The rise of the current development is driven by the underlying digital platform. Moore's law declared that a unit of computer processing power was halved in price every two years. Now we need a new "law" that explains how fast the price of bandwidth and storage is dropping. My educated guess is that the speed is nearly double that of Moore's law.

This is a revolution. We are moving from the economics of atoms to the economics of bits.

When something turns digital, it enters the economics of bits and is no longer restricted by the rules of the economics of atoms. In the economics of atoms, everything must be paid for; the transactions are more or less linear. In the economics of bits, the primary price is zero or next to zero. The money will still have to be paid out one way or another, but not as directly as before.

The economics of bits introduces a brand-new quality. When something becomes digital, it becomes free—free in cost, and often in price, too. Think about Angry Birds, recently the most downloaded digital game in dozens of countries. You can download its 600 or something little games free or for 99 cents, depending on the operator you use.

A multibillion-dollar industry is being created while you are reading this report. Look at the $500 billion price tag that *Forbes* put on Facebook. The Linux ecosystem is said to be worth $30 billion. Google has more than 24,000 employees and 6,000 offices, and it runs a business of around 4 billion inquiries a day. Remember, these figures are based on the logic of free.

However, we need to dig deeper if we are to comprehend the differences between the two economies. There are four novel types of logic that are emerging, especially online.

These four novel online business logics were described by bestselling author Chris Anderson:

1. *Direct cross-subsidies.* This is an old way to promote sales: get the first product for free, but pay for the second. Your office coffee machine is free, but the coffee costs (a lot).
2. *Three-party market.* In the primary relationship, the producer provides her services to the customers free. In the secondary relationship, an advertiser pays the producer for ad space. The more popular the service is, the higher the price.
3. *Freemium.* The basic service is free, but if you want a more advanced version with more features, you will have to pay. For instance, Spotify offers unlimited access to more than 10 million songs for free. However, the

customers, at the moment approximately one million people, pay a monthly subscription for listening on a smartphone, removing ads and services alike.

4. *Nonmonetary markets.* Human genes are apparently not only selfish. People do share and contribute for a wide range of personal reasons, such as reputation, participation, and a good time. Just think of the 12 million articles that make up Wikipedia.

MILLISECONDS MATTER

On May 6, 2010, at around 2:42 p.m. New York time, the world's most watched stock market index, the Dow Jones Industrial Average, went into free fall for almost five minutes and dropped 573 points, only to return nearly as quickly—it had gained 543 points by 3:07 p.m.

To give a couple of examples to explain what happened: shares of Procter & Gamble dropped more than one-third in minutes before recovering almost as quickly. Accenture saw its shares trade at a penny a share before closing the day at $42, not far from where they had begun it.

The day was afterward aptly named the "flash crash." It temporarily wiped out more than half a trillion U.S. dollars of equity value.

The events of that day left certain questions unanswered: What really happened? And what is going on with the stock markets, and more widely in the economy?

Let us get the background right. Until the late 1990s, stock trading was a straightforward affair, like what we have seen in the movies. Buyers and sellers gathered on floors, haggled until they agreed on a price, and completed the deal.

Then everything changed. U.S. regulators opened the stock markets to electronic trading. Anybody who had access to the Internet could connect to the exchange and execute an order.

Algorithmic trading was born. It is widely used by pension funds, mutual funds, and other investor-driven institutional traders to manage market impact and risk. It is commonly used in various investments strategies, such as:

- *Trend following.* This technique uses market price calculations, moving averages, and channel breakthroughs to try to make sense of market moves and benefit from the long-term moves that seem to take place.
- *Arbitrage.* This technique is widely used in economics and finance to take advantage of price differences between two or more markets.
- *Pair trading.* This is statistical arbitrage that enables traders to profit from movements (up, down, or sideways) in the markets.
- *Delta-neutral strategies.* These describe a portfolio of related financial securities in which the portfolio value remains unchanged despite small changes in the value of underlying securities.
- *Mean reversion.* This is a mathematical methodology applied to stock investing. The idea is that both a stock's high and its low are temporary, and it will tend to have and return to an average price over time. If the current price is below the average price, the stock is attractive for purchase, and vice versa.

I estimate that in any developed market, close to 80 percent of all trades are associated with algorithms. This means

that automated transactions are made at lightning speed. The financial markets are becoming more efficient, but this creates a risk that small mistakes can turn into catastrophes. And this is what I believe happened on May 7.

Moreover, algorithm-related developments are taking place everywhere on the Internet, not just on stock markets or next to them. In my mind, there is no doubt that web search engines have emerged as one of the central applications on the Internet. In fact, search has become the most significant activity that people engage in on the Internet. It is not just that the Internet is recognized as the number one source of information. A growing number of organizations depend on web search engines for their businesses.

Novel kinds of businesses have been created.

Stock traders saw an opportunity created by the opening of electronic trading. They figured out that if they brought mathematicians into the business, they could build powerful algorithms that would scan markets, spot trends, and find new opportunities in milliseconds. Today, these professionals are called high-frequency traders. They use brute computer power to move faster than any human being could to execute orders, book profits, and get out before anybody even figures out what has happened.

Maybe black-box trading or robotrading is a more accurate name than algorithmic trading. In the end, the computer algorithm decides on the timing, price, or quantity of the order, in many cases initiating the order without human intervention. In my opinion, this is the reason for the May 7 events.

The high-speed business makes thousands of trades a second and holds them for only a few minutes. The medium-speed business trades into and out of shares in about a second and holds them for two or three days.

Also the competition between algorithmic traders takes place in milliseconds. It is all about whose server is located closest to the source of trading data. Companies can capitalize on tiny differences in time, and the difference can be worth millions of dollars.

What we described is not relevant just to stock markets and the people involved with them. It affects and shapes our whole economy. The times of *I, Robot* are getting closer.

The Leadership Dilemmas

MANAGEMENT IS NOT A PROGRESSIVE SCIENCE. IF IT WERE, some sunny day, we would have the perfect theory of management. This is, of course, nonsense. In reality, leadership theories revolve around a specific set of dilemmas. These dilemmas don't change; they are more or less eternal. The answers will often be new ones, reflecting a changing business environment, but the relevant questions are the same. This chapter presents the dilemmas and the answers when they meet the future.

More than a hundred years ago, being the CEO of a newspaper in the United States just required "gorilla management" because making money was so easy that a monkey could do it—or so it was said. Most markets were growing fast; however, it was the golden era of the moguls and capitalism. "What is good for General Motors is good for the country" was an idea that many people accepted. Today, the life of a CEO is different. According to a recent Gallup survey, people rank business executives below lawyers, bankers, and newspaper reporters when it comes to honesty and ethical standards. They are

not trusted a lot. (Nurses are at the top of the ranking, by the way.) Capitalism and private enterprise have lost their gloss, at least for now. Even free marketers such as Alan Greenspan, the former head of the Federal Reserve, have apologized for their ideological zeal and admitted that more regulation is called for. In the emerging economies, by contrast, state ownership of big companies is common, as are huge conglomerates—and it works. Will the old days ever come back in the West?

Management ideas and books on the subject will always get inspiration from success. The "lean" concept came from Japan's success in the 1980s, and entrepreneurial ideas came from Silicon Valley. What's next? Our guess is management concepts from Asia, and particularly from China. One concept that could be imported to the West would be: "Be brave and invest for the long term; 20 years from now is like tomorrow."

Most management books and consultants don't talk about dilemmas; they give just one solution, one truth, or one answer. Well, the basic thing in leadership is uncertainty—decisions must be made before the future has arrived and before you know how the market will develop. Nobody knows for certain, but, as mentioned earlier, the discussion here will center on the dilemmas. These are some of the important dilemmas facing almost all companies and organizations, and the answers that result when they are confronted with the trends outlined in the other chapters.

THE LOYALTY DILEMMA

1. The CEO must stay totally loyal to the board and the owners; his job is to maximize money for the shareholders. Forget the other so-called stakeholders. That's why

CEOs are paid well when shares go up and why the
president and the CEO should be the same person.

2. The CEO develops the strategy, and she gets the laurels
if it works well and is fired if it doesn't. Her loyalty is to
all stakeholders, including employees and customers—
not just the owners and the board. The board and the
CEO have different roles in the company.

At present, most members of top management are compensated (often very well compensated) to ensure their total loyalty
to one of the stakeholders: the owners. The trend over the past
20 years has proved this. Even during the economic crisis, top
management compensation grew at the same time as a lot of
employees were fired.

This is the situation right now, but the trends indicate a
change. Employees are better educated, their respect for authority is coming down, and they don't want to be seen as human
machines that can be disposed of when it is deemed expedient.
The owners today are institutional investors and hedge funds
that are looking for short-term profits; they are buying today
and selling tomorrow, whereas employees want the company
to exist for many years. Most shareholders are speculators, and
that is OK (making money is not forbidden), but don't call
them owners. In the old days, when shares were a long-term
investment, you really felt that you were an owner and that you
had some responsibility for your company. Nowadays, shares
are a commodity. This situation will not last; we can expect a
new balance, with the best employees leaving "for-short-term-
profit" companies in favor of more responsible ones. That will
force CEOs and boards to listen carefully to the employees and
other stakeholders and thus broaden their loyalties so that loyalty to owners is just one of them.

When that happens, the United States will be following the continental European tradition. In most European companies, the CEO is not a member of the board. The board is the overseer; it approves the CEO's strategic plan and is responsible for that plan's execution and success.

The trend in ownership would be toward long-term investment in a company that you trust and believe in. However, the trend is indeed a long-term one. The much-talked-about tax on stock exchange transactions could put a premium on responsibility and punish short-termism. The loyalty dilemma raises a basic question about the future of private businesses, and indeed of capitalism as we know it.

THE HIERARCHY DILEMMA

1. A centralized system of decision making works best in any company. A steep hierarchy is needed, especially in a fast-changing business environment, and it is always changing. Decisions must be taken where the information is available: at the top level.

2. A decentralized company works best. A flat hierarchy provides energy and innovation and empowers employees; it ensures that there are more eyes and ears available to watch trends develop.

The military is the archetypical hierarchical organization. You can immediately see who is in charge: it is the guy with the most stars on his shoulder. In companies, a black suit and a big office with thick carpets may indicate who the boss is, but in some companies (most likely the decentralized ones), everyone wears blue jeans and you don't know who

the boss is. Will hierarchies become steeper or flatter in the future?

The reasons for the steep hierarchy are obvious. Decisions should be taken where the best and most comprehensive information is available, and that is at the top. At a lower level in the organization, solid facts are available, but they are by definition only partial; people do not have the big picture. However, a centralized organization requires a reliable flow of information; without it, the company does not have the complete overall picture, and that is a dangerous situation for employees, too.

Today's business environment is changing fast; you need a lot of eyes and ears to watch developments. Top management in big organizations often sits at the center of a bureaucracy, protected from the outside world. We can all think of several examples of CEOs who failed to react to obvious signals from the market. They are not the first to discover a new trend in the marketplace or in technology. The salespeople could be the ones to listen to. That is why you need to decentralize, to change all employees from "well-oiled cogs" to people in positions of real responsibility. This also provides motivation, and motivated employees are a strong asset in any company. The ideal CEO would be a coordinator or a facilitator. This is exactly what a lot of companies are moving toward today. Decisions should be taken at the lowest level possible to ensure motivation and real-world knowledge.

We need a completely new organization chart. The "moment of truth" occurs when the company meets the customer, whether offline or online. That's when your product or service is accepted or rejected. That is where the real top managers are found, those with the best and most recent information. They should be put at the top of the chart. Michael Porter introduced the concept of the "value chain." In his model, it ends with the

customer. On the contrary, this is where it begins; what the customer values is the real value of the product, regardless of the costs that were added on its way to the customer. That puts the CEO at the bottom of the chart—the person who is farthest away from the moment of truth and thus the start of the value chain. The CEO may be the formal decision maker, but the real bosses are those who have a daily dialogue with customers. The information must trickle down from them to the CEO, undiluted. This chart is the opposite of what we see today; it may offend managers (and the board members, because they are further down), but it will empower the rest of the organization. It will inspire a lot of innovation and perhaps remove some bureaucracy. Why isn't it done? Because the bottleneck is where bottlenecks are on bottles: at the top. My advice: try it and watch what happens. Turn the organization chart upside down.

THE VALUE DILEMMA

1. Control costs, results, and performance. Having a lot of data on employee performance gives top management the best tools for responsible leadership.
2. It's about motivating the employees and empowering them. Control turns employees into potential thieves of company time. The decentralized, value-oriented company is the future, if not the present.

Are the company and its results driven by the enthusiasm of the employees—their belief in its values, interesting work, and challenges—or are they interested only in the pay? Surveys tell us that in the Nordic countries, work values are mostly social; it's the camaraderie. In the United States, the employees are

driven by the paycheck, not by motivation. Numerous studies tell us that money does not motivate people in the long run. A raise is soon taken for granted, and a new raise is expected.

The dilemma is this: control or motivation, money or values, hard versus soft, mind versus heart. It's an old dilemma. It started with the theory of scientific management.

The idea behind scientific management is this: what you don't measure and don't control does not happen. If you don't measure performance, but rely only on "motivation," it will not work. If you don't know whether this office or this employee is performing better than another, you cannot reward those who get the best results. It provides us with the tools to measure who gets the job done and who doesn't. This is not "Big Brother is watching you." When you work long hours and get a lot of work done, then you want to be rewarded for it. You have people in every company who are doing nothing (well, not doing the things they are paid to do), and they will go on doing nothing or doing other things if you don't monitor their performance. Control is welcome to the majority, the hard-working employees.

The reason for soft is this: scientific management was invented for the factory floor, for manual work. It was easy to measure how many clutches this section of the assembly line delivered. It was never intended for the office. How many good ideas have you had today? How many colleagues have you assisted today? How many smiles have you given away today? You can measure the number of hours you have been sitting at your desk or the number of memos you have sent, but that is meaningless. If you try to measure things of this kind, your employees will just concentrate on what is measured and forget everything else. At the same time, you will demotivate people. There is only one way of ensuring that everybody is

doing his best. That's values, or having a value-driven organiza-tion. Use narratives; tell employees what the company is about, and turn them into believers in company values. You can even control this; just ask staff members whether they are thriving and whether they feel good about what they are doing. Happy employees get the best results. Not all CEOs are charismatic enough to motivate all people, but they can call for help from colleagues, books, or even consultants. A lot of companies do have "core values," but in most cases employees either are not persuaded or seduced by them or simply don't remember them. The so-called core values are mostly words without substance. Values are more than that.

THE SENSE-MAKING DILEMMA

1. To find meaning (the answer to the basic question: why do we exist?) is perhaps the biggest challenge a CEO faces. We use and develop stories in order to live our lives as a continuum; if we cannot place an event or a piece of information within a narrative that is relevant for us, it loses its meaning. Find your company story and stick to it.
2. In real life, only a few CEOs have the emotional intel-ligence required to nurture the company story. Such a story may be a good thing, but most companies thrive nicely without a story to develop the company.

More than 24 million people have read the short bestseller *Who Moved My Cheese?* It's a business book about mice in a maze and their quest to find cheese. It is not a children's book; it is about change management, and it motivates employees

to accept change. Its strength is in the narrative. It is irresistible; narratives are actually the best persuaders on earth. That is why stories have been told for millennia. Since this is the case, all companies should use them.

The fact that CEOs don't use narratives more than they do is not because they are stupid; it is because they are clever. They have degrees from management schools—MBAs and the like. They learn to become rational; they forget the human side of management. The classic example in change management is this. The CEO informs all employees about the company's restructuring; all the facts are presented. However, the employees think (rightly or wrongly) that there is some sinister motive behind the change. They believe that the company is not doing as badly as the CEO claimed. Change is not really needed, they think. Change management works when employees are positive and look forward to the change; otherwise, it will fail. The mice book tells a story about the need to look for cheese, even if it entails change. It tells the postchange story—the outcome, not the process. You are seduced; you forget that mice and humans are different, and you forget that it is a story, it didn't happen—it is fiction. But it works.

A company is a tribe, and its members are both emotional and rational—like all of us. In the evening, we are seduced by a film. We know that what we are seeing is not true. It is happening on a screen; the actors are not really in love, and they don't die—they just pretend. Still, we laugh or cry because it is true in our heart. If it works in the evening, why should it not work while you are at your job? Should we lie to our employees? No, of course not. The mouse story is not a lie; it is a story for the heart, and it becomes true in your heart when you finish the book. A good story motivates you in the right direction. Today's managers need story power.

Some CEOs are storytellers, but most are not; it is not in their DNA. When they need it, they can buy advice from outside or ask their colleagues for help. As with all things in life, there are rules in storytelling, rules that ensure that a story is compelling. Here are some simple, basic rules for the good story:

1. Believe strongly in your narrative—if you don't, others won't either.
2. There must be some challenge, some problem to overcome, but it is *how* you win that matters. By which values do you overcome the challenge? This is the essence of the story, the moral—what should be learned from it. In movies, the protagonist often wins because of honesty, love, or courage. The antagonist is typically just fighting for personal gain. Remember Robin Hood—he would steal, but he was stealing from the rich and giving to the poor.
3. Walk the talk. Tell a story about deeds and actions, about people (or mice), not about some abstract words like "company core values." The persuasive narrative is lacking in words like "respect for the individual." Tell a story about a particular employee by name. Tell how he acted with genuine respect for a colleague.

The founders of a company will be able to tell a passionate story about what the company is about. The problem often arises with the next generation, when professional management takes over. The new managers should study what the founders believed in and tell it again. The three principles are easy to learn, but they are often forgotten in daily life, especially the first one. If you don't believe strongly in what you are saying,

forget it. Read your annual report: does it tell about a major challenge and the values and effort that led to the good result? Please, introduce a little passion.

If you are running your company as if the employees were materialist rationalists, you have a problem. The company is a tribe. We want to work for social reasons, to accomplish something, not just for money. Money will retain employees, but it does not motivate them, not even a bonus for a profitable year. Next year, such a bonus will be taken for granted, and it will be a negative if it does not come. Postmaterialist employees will soon become the majority, and they ask for *meaning*: why are we doing this, and how? That is why companies donate to charity—to prove that they have a heart and put their values into action. Your story should be about meaning. All companies have a story, and all companies have values. The problem is that many of them are shallow and hidden. Usually, the stories are about becoming the largest company or the market leader—the winner. A good narrative tells *how* to become the winner—the values that enabled us to win. It could be working hard, ethics, research, innovation, or a good strategy. Tell the story in three steps:

1. First everything was nice and peaceful.
2. Then we were challenged—by the competition or otherwise—and we acted to deal with the situation. It was not easy, but eventually we won by these values.
3. Everything is nice and peaceful again—ready for the next challenge.

The story of the mice follows this pattern, as do all profitable movies, because it is basic; it is how we experience life and understand it; it is eternal.

Is your company like a theater, and are your customers the audience? The CEO writes the script and the employees are the actors, and if the performance is a good one, the customers will applaud. Let us explain how it could be done; the parallel between the theater (we have chosen a classic, the world-famous Cinderella story) and the company is clear:

+ *The protagonist.* In any play, the protagonist is the one we identify with, the one we hope will reach her goal (Cinderella). In your company, it must be your customers. The better you know the wishes and dreams of your customers, the better you will sell.
+ *The helper(s).* In most, if not all, plays, we have one or more helpers (the birds and the mice in the Cinderella story). The helper(s) will identify with the protagonist and stay loyal, whatever happens. This is your role as a company. You win by identifying with the dreams of your customers.
+ *The antagonist* (the evil stepmother). For you as a company, the antagonist is the things that prevent you from reaching your goal; it could be poor service or high prices. Remember, it is never your competitors. The antagonist could be inside your company—poor quality control, for example.
+ *The fairy godmother.* The fairy godmother helps Cinderella, albeit in a more miraculous way than the helpers. For the company, it could be a "special offer" or some innovative way to satisfy your customers' dreams.
+ *The Holy Grail.* This is the dream; it is what your customers really want. This is Prince Charming. If your company knows the secret of customer satisfaction, you will become the preferred helper.

The good story about your company values must start with the customer: the protagonist. Discover the true story about a time when your customer needed something, and, with these values, you delivered, in spite of all these things. Such narratives exist somewhere in your organization; you will have to do some "story mining" to select the true ones and make them your company stories or narratives.

The story may be written down, but the best place for it is inside your mind and your heart: "story living" could be the goal. Furthermore, the story is a living thing; it must be dynamic, and it must add new aspects to the core story.

THE GLOBALIZATION DILEMMA

1. You need to go global, or you will lose to the companies and organizations that do. These are globalization times; the window is open for the next 10 years. Use it to invest overseas; only the big companies with a global reach will survive.

2. The doors are only partly open; there are still a lot of political risks, legal and cultural barriers. Furthermore, outsourcing may be short-lived, and the "global consumer" does not exist. The vast majority of companies must rely on their home market. Stay local and rely on markets and customers that you know well.

The period between 1870 and 1914 was an especially good one for international companies. The national economies were open; foreign companies and products were welcome. The Great Depression that started in 1929 unleashed a wave of barriers to the free flow of international trade. Since World War II,

these barriers have been removed—not all of them, but most of them in areas other than agricultural products.

The future belongs to companies that are operating in many countries, both mature and emerging economies—the more the better. The reason, as we all know, is economies of scale. Today production and research can move to countries where costs are low, and global companies are better positioned to do just that: they can move around, and they have the knowledge to do so. Small may be beautiful, but business is not a beauty contest.

Globalization may be the right thing to do, but the issue is complicated. Perhaps a few hundred companies can prosper in a global market because they are selling commodities—standardized products and services like oil, cars, telecommunication, raw materials, and shipping. The doors may be open, but the cultural differences are still huge, and they will not disappear soon, if they ever do. Corporate cultures are different; the rules and values for Scandinavia, the United States, and China or India are different. Furthermore, products must increasingly be adapted to suit the local culture and taste. These are barriers to globalization. Another barrier is the trend toward "buying local" because it is seen as safer and more friendly to the environment. This is a small but growing segment. The labor costs in China and India are going up—not as fast as the GDP, but almost. What is outsourced today may be insourced in the not too distant future. In the rich part of the world and for the new global middle class, we are seeing that segments are shrinking and mass markets are disappearing. The needs and aspirations of consumers are becoming more specialized and focused. Look at the market for magazines; it has gone from mass market to special interest. The markets for Ferrari cars and for magazines about mountain bikes in each country are

small, but globally they are big enough. We will see a lot of companies selling to small but globalized segments. This is not selling to some "global consumer" but finding a small global segment. This is likely to become the future of globalization. The other possibility is mass customization. The product is mass-produced, but it is adapted for numerous local markets based on local customs or individual tastes. Globalization? Yes, but in the long run it will be for reasons other than those given at present (labor costs and economies of scale).

THE OPENNESS DILEMMA

1. Listen to your employees and your customers. The more time you devote to "society," the less time you have to run your business. "Shared value" and corporate social responsibility (CSR) are nice words, but charity is a personal thing; companies contribute already by serving a market.

2. The transparent company is open to and part of the society it serves. No company is an island. It has a dialogue with all its stakeholders, including the social media. Soon the company will be judged as if it were a person, a friend. The consumer will ask: "Do I like the way this company behaves? Is it a friend, or is it just some narcissistic and greedy entity without a conscience?"

The company is an island in the sense that its responsibility is toward its customers. It is not responsible to "society" or to the social media. The PR department may try to influence the media to create a good impression so as to avoid negative

reactions from customers and regulators. If you are a clean tech company, it is a good thing for you to lobby for green issues, but otherwise time devoted to a dialogue with society is time that is not used for the things that you are paid to do—like running the company. These are yesterday's answers to the dilemma.

The modern and especially the future-oriented response is this: companies are part of society, just as all citizens are. Schools, universities, infrastructure, and law and order are supporting your company. To say that you need corporate social responsibility is stating the obvious. Any expert in communications can tell you: tell the truth, the whole truth, and nothing but the truth. If you don't, then the media will draw their own conclusions. If you send a press release claiming environmental reasons for this or that decision, but you are doing it just to make more money, the press will find out; instead, tell the press the truth about profitability, and they will write that at the same time, your decision will benefit the environment. More and more whistle-blowers and organizations like WikiLeaks will talk; it is better that you do it first. Secrecy is no longer possible. Your employees will respect a transparency policy; they are citizens as well. You may still get away with lies and half-truths today, but soon it will become impossible. Build a reputation for honesty—you may need it on a rainy day.

THE SOCIAL ORGANIZATION DILEMMA

1. Any company is a social organization, and access to information is the key to success. The analogy is viruses; they spread like information. So, stay close to where the most viruses (information) are. Information is king.

2. The other possibility is comparisons. Compare the advantages of spontaneity and intuitive decision making with those of planning and the systematic approach. Compare and conclude.

For the very few people who have had the time and energy to read Nietzsche's book *Thus Spake Zarathustra*, this may be what they remember: Zarathustra decides to return to his village after years of meditation in the mountains. He believes that he has resolved all the big issues, but in the village he notices that he has to re-resolve them—this time with the people. Information and knowledge are created through dialogue.

For ages, the main vehicles that people used to create knowledge and understanding were analogies and metaphors. Every time a new analogy or metaphor was added to the world, the common body of knowledge was increased. For example, information was seen as a virus.

Viruses have an extremely long history, and they are widespread on our planet. They are the simplest organisms, consisting of genetic information and mechanisms for transferring this information. A common way of comprehending viruses is to see them as pieces of information. Actually, their existence is informationally dependent and constrained. They cannot exist alone. They can exist only in relationship to another organism. Without this, they will cease to exist. Similarly, seemingly independent people are connected by information in such a way that they are no longer independent and separable from each other.

It is no wonder that in organizations, the favorite position seems to be as close as possible to the CEO or the president. Being close to information is what really matters.

All human operations, whether we are talking about transportation networks, power transfer, or cooperation among people, have plenty of essential characteristics. However, the most important ones have to do with facilitating beneficial relationships.

Maybe the time of traditional organizations is over. Think about WikiLeaks; it is not even correct to call it an organization. After all, it has no paid staff, no office, no address, and no corporate number.

Besides, the "CEO," Julian Assange, does not have a home. He has traveled from country to country and stayed with friends and supporters. The organization exists wherever he goes. It is maintained by hundreds or even thousands of volunteers who participate in small or larger ways. It is estimated that WikiLeaks has only four or five full-time workers. We know only two of them by name; the other key members are referred to only by initials: K, L, and M, for instance.

In a fast, digital, and highly competitive world, we should seriously rethink organizations from the viewpoint of interconnectivity. WikiLeaks is not the only organization to have achieved notable results with scarce resources. Many have done so, from al-Qaida to Facebook.

We also learn by using comparisons, or dichotomies, to put it more finely. We compare two different management philosophies and claim that they result in different behaviors.

First, Google's management principles have been described like this:

1. Ideas come from anywhere. Encourage the generation of new ideas.
2. Share everything you can. Work on success/failure stories to create synergies.

3. "You are brilliant." Smart people like to work with smart people. Always find a place for a smart person.
4. Let people pursue their dreams. People work better on issues that excite them.
5. Look for progress, not for perfection. Get things out in the market to develop and improve them with your customers, not vice versa.
6. Data are apolitical. Base all your decisions on data. Only sound ideas will rise to the top.
7. Creativity loves constraints. Make everyone aware of them to reach your creativity potential.
8. Focus on users, not on money. If the users get what they want, money will follow.
9. Don't kill projects. Morph them, reevaluate them, and relaunch them.

Second, for the sake of learning, I present five principles of management adapted from Henry Mintzberg, with my comments:

1. Manage the bottom line (as if you make money by managing money).
2. Make a plan for every action (no spontaneity, please; no learning).
3. Move managers around to be certain that they never get to know anything but management well (and kick the boss upstairs—it's better to manage a portfolio than to manage a real business).
4. Always be objective, which means treating people as objects (in particular, hire and fire employees the way you buy and sell machines—everything is a "portfolio").
5. Do everything in five easy steps.

What thoughts come to your mind when you compare the two lists? I think that if you follow the five-step program, you can bring down any lucrative business, or even an industry, in 10 years.

THE PERFECT LEADER

In 10, 20, 50, or even 100 years, leadership will revolve around the same dilemmas, but this will not stop the avalanche of management books. This may be a good thing, but most of these books forget that even business leaders are human—most of them, that is. Perfection does not exist in the real world. The ideal CEO should be a people person, show empathy, and make tough decisions. She should also be visionary and supervise the cash flow. She should adapt the company to face the future and make sure that the results for this quarter are positive. She must talk to the board, to employees, to suppliers, to customers, to accountants, and to regulators, and have a family life that is full of love, peace, and understanding. She should take time to engage in sports to stay fit. And, don't forget: she should read management books.

7

The Authors' Conclusion

THE WORLD BANK ESTIMATES THAT BY 2025, SIX EMERGING economies alone will account for more than half of all global growth. The World Bank also projects that as a group, emerging economies will on average grow 4.7 percent between 2011 and 2025. Mature economies are forecast to grow by 2.3 percent over the same period—only half as much. We have the slow-growing West and the fast-growing East. The East is catching up. How can we explain this big disparity? Our conclusion is clear.

Economic growth is dream-driven. It is not driven by governments but by all of us; call it "people dreams." When people really want something, they will do their best to acquire it. When the majority really wants something, when it has a dream, then high economic growth happens. The emerging economies are growing twice as fast as the mature ones. It seems that the Western dream today has become less strong than the Eastern one. This is because North America, Western Europe, and Japan have been able to satisfy most of people's

material needs. One dream has been fulfilled, and we are waiting for the next one; the West is between dreams. A decline in
economic growth is not inevitable; it happens when dreams
fade or are forbidden. The emerging economies have high
growth because their dream (a material one) is strong. If the
West could discover a new dream, it would grow just as fast as
the East.

The West is defined as the mature economies in North
America, Europe, Japan, Australia, and New Zealand—the
low-growth area. The East is the emerging economies of Asia
and Latin America—the high-growth area.

EASTERN DREAMS

When China and India were poor, they had an ideological
vision, the political idea of working toward some ideal social
structure. The same can be said of Brazil and Russia. They put
values before money and ideology before profit. There was,
however—as history has clearly shown us—no shared vision
between the ideological governments and their citizens; governments promoted an ideology, but the people wanted higher
income, a car, and a house. That's what they are getting now,
and this is why their economies are growing fast—their governments allow and promote a shared vision. This shared vision
is about material wealth and higher incomes. The power of the
people has been unleashed, with stunning results. The material
dream is strong in the East. Work comes before family. Work is
more important than vacations and shorter working hours. The
goal is wealth, and people are prepared to strive patiently for it,
even though it does not happen in a single year. They are, however, experiencing fast progress over the course of their lives.

When GDP grows 10 percent per year, wealth doubles in seven years. When the people and the government share a dream, the result is high trust in institutions. In surveys, 88 percent of Chinese people say that they trust their government. Trust in financial institutions is also high, at 90 percent.

The East is just now going through an extremely materialistic era, and this is not surprising when the recent past was poverty—many people will still remember it. This is a Golden Age for the East because there is a promise of ever-increasing wealth.

WESTERN DREAMS

During the 1950s and until the end of the 1960s, the material dream was very much alive in the West. It was about a car, a house, and education for the children—about getting rich and about consumption. In this period, economic growth was high, and trust in public institutions was high. In 1965, 80 percent of people said in surveys that they trusted that the government was heading in the right direction. This was the peak year for trust in the United States (much the same as in present-day China). This was the Golden Age in the West (not just the United States) because the government and the people were in agreement about the direction of the country. Recent figures show that trust has declined to just 40 percent. The materialistic dream has faded; work is still important, but not as much as it was, and certainly not as much a priority as it is in the East. The result is lower growth.

Japan had high growth rates until 1990—its people got rich, and that was what they wanted and needed. Since then, economic growth has been much lower; the economy ran out

of steam, and there was no new vision. When a nation reaches a certain stage (around $20,000 to $30,000 per capita), something vital happens: the economy and a higher income are still relevant, but other things in life (nonmaterial values, that is) are becoming equally important. We sometimes call this era of the mature economies "postmodern." The prefixes *post* and *non* say it all: there is no vision and no dream; just the message that the past is no more. The West and Japan have reached this stage; it is time for renewal, for a new vision and strategy. We call Western economies mature. *Mature* implies that they have reached a certain age; they are seen as satisfied or even complacent.

THE WEST BETWEEN DREAMS

Is the West between dreams? What does this mean, and how can we explain it? Two internationally noted theorists can help us. The first is Dr. Ichak Adizes, an advisor to governments and companies for many years. The second is Joseph Campbell, who invented the modern theory of storytelling and its relationship to our daily life.

Adizes compares a human life with the life of a company, or indeed any institution. We start as young persons, curious, looking for possibilities, action-oriented, willing to try something new, and challenging conventional wisdom. When we get older, we take fewer risks, and our desire for change disappears. Older people prefer clear, fixed rules of behavior. The same general rule applies to companies, says Adizes. There are exceptions to this rule, of course; people as well as companies can reinvent themselves and avoid the ossification that would otherwise be the result. Have Western societies become old

without having reinvented themselves? Have they ossified? The question has to be addressed. Our answer is yes for most of the West; for the United States, the answer is a cautious yes, but still a yes. What about your company?

Joseph Campbell describes the human life as a constant interaction between what he calls "order" and "movement." Order is when life is quiet and in harmony; movement is when life is about striving for some result, some goal. Campbell compares this with the life of the hunter/gatherer in ancient times. The hunter would hunt in the jungle; it was dangerous, but the prize was worth it. When he returned to his tribe with his deer, it was time for him to leave the period of movement and return to the universe of order. This is the eternal interaction between movement and order, between danger and rest. We all experience it in our daily life: the peaceful time after a long and eventful working day.

Both order and movement are needed in life. If we had only order, we would lead a life of quiet desperation. If we had only movement and change, we would get desperate and demand order and rest. After a long period of movement (the material era), we are back in the order universe, resting and in harmony. After some time, human beings will want to go hunting again—we will have a longing for the movement universe and discovering new dreams. The era of harmony will not last. That applies to people as well as nations.

THE EAST AND THE WEST IN GLOBALIZATION

When Jules Verne's fictional character Phileas Fogg traveled around the globe more than 100 years ago, he needed 80 days

to complete his journey; today, it can be done in 24 hours. Look at the globe as shrinking from the size of a tennis ball to the size of a pea. We can comprehend the business world only if we act globally. The key to making sense of the future of business is the central competition-collaboration relationship between the East and the West. We have to understand our relationships for this reason and because international trade is growing, in most years twice as fast as global GDP. We are one business world today, with 20 percent of all products crossing an international border. Rudyard Kipling (1865–1936), the English Nobel Prize winner in literature, once wrote: "East is East and West is West, and never the twain [two] shall meet." He was a man of the Victorian age, and he was right then, but is he really right today? Commercially, he is obviously wrong, but when we look at values (what people see as good and what they see as bad; what they praise and condemn), Kipling is still right; we *do* have different values. But we would expect to find that the gap between the East and the West is closing because of growing global trade and communication. Eventually, we would expect to end up with common values. However, the figures from the World Value Survey tell us that the gap is *not* closing, or even getting smaller; we will have to live with it, perhaps for the rest of this century. That's why it is important to identify and understand these differences in values.

Furthermore, our values are changing—slowly, but they are changing in the same direction. We are walking in the same direction at the same speed; we won't meet. So, don't expect the need for understanding to go away. Our visions, dreams, and values are not the same; businesses are globalizing, but our values are not.

We are always learning from and imitating successful business leaders; we read books by them and about them—how

do they do it, what are their secrets? (Remember the books on Japanese management?) Tomorrow the most successful business leaders will be coming from the high-growth economies of the East. The West is in desperate need of a new vision, while the East is already living one.

Growth (economic and otherwise) is a natural thing; it is very human, and it is the result of many people working hard for some goal. The politicians want us to believe that they can bring growth. They can't; all they can do is listen to their citizens. Legislation is a helper at best, not the driving force for growth. Growth is high when people believe that something is really important to them. When their dream is to own their house and to have a car, they will work hard, but when it is about buying a second house or a second car, this may still be a desirable thing to wish for, but it is not a vital dream—they will tend to pursue other goals in life as well. Dreams in the West are slowly but surely moving away from material things.

Henry Ford once said: "If I had asked my customers what they wanted, they would have said a faster horse." This is exactly what governments and other leaders in the West are offering their people today: a faster horse. Well, that's not entirely true; governments and companies are also concerned about the environment, the climate, nature, and ethics, but this is a timid beginning. Profit before values is going to change to values before profit. It has begun. Cities are getting green; sustainability is the rule in most projects: wind power and electric cars. Corporate Social Responsibility (CSR) is being talked about and increasingly becoming part of company strategy. This is the beginning: a timid one, but it augurs the coming values transformation. This is not a no-growth thing; it is just growth in industries other than the present ones. Are companies and customers in the West ready?

Many people are waiting for it to happen, but it is a difficult change of logic. Never before in history has the majority of the population not had to worry about the next meal, or simply having enough to satisfy basic human needs. Only two or three generations have had the luxury of having enough. Of course, we still buy stuff, but shopping is no longer about alleviating some material need; it is more like a leisure activity. The West is waiting for the next dream. Expect it to come gradually, and not as a common dream, but as millions of individual dreams, although with a common theme. In the materialist age, people wanted to own a house and a car. Now they want to own their lives and to choose their path in life themselves. This is an exciting future, full of inspiration and diversity.

The figures on the values gap between the East and the West illustrate this trend. For the next 10 years, the challenge is mostly for the mature economies. The figures are based on surveys conducted by Geert Hofstede, the highly respected pioneer of the study of intercultural cooperation.

THE UNITED STATES AND CHINA: THE DIFFERENT VALUE PATTERNS

Studies of social norms in different countries indicate that the United States scores high on *indulgence,* as measured by happiness, the importance of leisure, thriving, and being in control of your life. China scores high on *restraint,* reflecting a belief that indulgence must be curbed and regulated by strict social norms. The conclusion is that the United States and the rest of the West have reached a high level of wealth, and that's why people can afford to pursue other dreams as well. In China and other emerging economies, restraint is the

price that people willingly pay in order to get rich. The same difference is observed if we look at *long-term versus short-term orientation*. A long-term orientation values perseverance, thrift, and sustained efforts toward slow results. A short-term orientation values quick results. The United States is short-term, while China is long-term. Again, in China, there is a willingness to wait for results—the dream is worth waiting for because it is all-important. That's not so in the West. The West is pursuing different goals, including nonmaterial ones, but people expect results this year, not in 10 years.

One more difference between East and West is *individualism* versus *collectivism*. In the United States, you can pursue individual dreams; you are responsible for your own life and your immediate family, but that's all. In China, you are a member of a larger and more permanent structure or group; you are less on your own. The *power distance* in organizations points in the same direction. In China, the hierarchy is steep—you follow the leader. In the United States, you follow the leader only as long as it makes sense to you.

Only in one respect do China and the United States have similar values. They are both *masculine* societies. Recognition and challenges are more important than good working relationships and employment security. (This is just about values; men can have feminine values and women masculine ones. It is about social values, not gender roles.)

For the next 10 to 15 years, the East has a dream to fulfill, higher income, and this is exactly what the governments are trying to help people attain. In the West, things are a lot more complicated. As we have seen, an increasing number of people are pursuing nonmaterial goals in life. Interestingly, *Americans tend to trust the less material professions the most*. On top of the trusted list are teachers, middle-class people, people who run

small businesses, and military officers. At the bottom of the list are car dealers, CEOs of large corporations, stockbrokers, and lawyers. Specifically, 84 percent of Americans trust teachers, while only 23 percent trust CEOs of large corporations, in spite of the fact that there are four times more public relations employees in companies than there are news editors and reporters.

If you ask Americans whether *today's young people will have a better life than their parents*, a recent Gallup poll says that 55 percent believe that this is very or somewhat unlikely. Only 44 percent say that it is likely. A slight majority are not optimistic about the long-term future. These figures are sending a message to us. The corresponding figures for China would look very different.

THE VALUES OF THE FUTURE

The West has fulfilled its dream about material wealth, and it is still looking for the next dream. This new dream is what a lot of people in the West are waiting for and searching for. What kind of dream is it? It is millions of dreams, individual ones and personal ones. In the East, the dream is about higher income and a better material life.

What is the future of values; where are they heading? If we extrapolate the trends, then the direction in clear:

- The hierarchy in organizations is getting flatter.
- There will be more individualization; you will pursue your own personal dreams.
- There will be more feminine values; relationships will be valued more than recognition.

* Ambiguity and uncertainty will be accepted more easily.
* Indulgence (and thus less restraint) is becoming more prevalent.

Values change slowly, but they do change, and Western societies have to adapt to them in order to improve the lives of their citizens and to have a more prosperous economy. We can summarize our findings in the five most important challenges facing companies and society. The challenges for the West and the East are different. We have to present one set of challenges for each.

THE BIG FIVE CHALLENGES
FOR THE WEST

1. *Emotionalize.* Since citizens in the West are increasingly postmaterialist, the message is clear: you need to appeal to hearts. We still need products, but they must have an emotional appeal—the product as such is becoming a by-product. The price of a T-shirt is determined by what is written on it, not by the shirt as such. Employees want to know why they are working; money is not the prime motivation. The company mission must be value-based. Profit is not the reason for company ownership; it is just the end result of activities. Employees expect to be told about values and connect to them; the company must be value-driven.

2. *Personalize.* Just as employees expect to be treated as individuals, so do customers. Products and services are still part of our self-portrait. Up until now, this has been a group portrait—the brand. It still is, but you have to

be able to make it personal; it must say something about you as an individual as well. Consumers will want to be involved and take part. Cocreation is an essential part of this.

3. *Decentralize.* Up until now, companies have become bigger, but brands are becoming smaller. Look at the craft brewery market. Perhaps ownership may still be concentrated in fewer hands, but the physical company, the unit of innovation, design, and production, will become smaller because of new technology and consumer demand and because employees want more responsibility. Smaller companies leave more room for this.

4. *Innovate.* Yes, everyone tells you to do so, but the challenges are huge: how do you address emotions and feelings? How can financial institutions like the big five adapt? How can the retail industry combine visits to the store and online shopping? Most of the innovative thinking has to be bold and happen far outside the box.

5. *Feminize.* Feminine values are entering the workplace; good relations are seen as more important for results, and the modern workplace is about building relationships, about people working together as teams. The business hero is becoming a team member. It is still about individualism, but the company is becoming more social.

THE BIG FIVE CHALLENGES FOR THE EAST

1. *Get ready for the next era.* In 10 to 15 years, many emerging countries will have reached an income of

$25,000 to $30,000 per person or will be getting close to that level. The challenges for the next era will be similar to the Big Five for the West.

2. *Infrastructure.* People are moving from rural areas into towns, and they need homes, heating, and electricity. Roads are needed to allow better transportation and distribution. This applies for all emerging economies. It is the era of the big international construction companies.

3. *Education.* As industry is in need of more scientists and as incomes go up, education will become one of the major growth industries. The challenge is to combine the old classroom with online education.

4. *Manufacturing.* The market for means of transportation is moving to the East. The East is expected to dominate this world market. Its huge home markets provide the advantage. The consumer electronics industry is also going to be dominated by companies from the East. They will be in the forefront of research as well. This is happening now, but it will continue, as domestic demand rises and exports to the rest of the world, including other emerging economies, increase.

5. *Automation.* When wages are rising (and they already are), the answer is automation.

THREE EXAMPLES FROM THE FUTURE

The economies of the West are service economies; 75 percent of their GDP comes from services, thanks to automation and globalization, and only 25 percent comes from industry, manufacturing, agriculture, and fisheries put together. In 10 years' time, the figure for services will reach 80 percent. Gradually,

our brains will become the sole tools we use at work. Of course, we will use our emotions, too. Few people touch real physical products during the day. The workplace has become nonmaterial, but we are longing for the material environment. Look at what is happening at home. When we are at home, we produce: that's the do-it-yourself market. We need to employ our muscles as well as our brains. We can replace the fitness hour with something real. Combine this with the trend toward individualism, together with new technology, and you have a new industry: the one-person factory. This is the new industry for personalized products. This is just one example to illustrate how a lot of people will discover their new dream. They will gladly leave their cubicle and the office hierarchy.

For centuries, humans have been told by society, by priests, by authorities, and by parents what to do and what to think. Now we want to become our own masters. Sometimes a revolution helps, sometimes a hierarchy is torn down, and sometimes you just do as you please, not what your parents wish you to do. This is individuality, bringing home responsibility for one's own life. A spiritual market is part of the answer. It may grow to the same size as the market for healthcare. Stress occurs when you are unable to say no and you have to do something that is not in accordance with your dream. Advising people how to "come home to your self" and how to discover your dream will become a major new industry. The need is already obvious. Is this a real industry? Well, as much as legal counseling is. It is a service that you will pay for.

Retail must expect slow growth in the years to come (at much the same rate as GDP, say 2.5 percent at most) if nothing new happens. It's a traditional industry with fierce price competition and today is being challenged by online stores, too. Expect a radical transformation: from products to dreams.

How do you sell dreams in a store? Some are already doing it. The store of the future will look more like a theater or a showroom; it will tell the customer (or rather the guest) how it can fulfill this or that emotional need (small or big). The old discount store will continue to exist, but the emotional market is the new thing. The retail industry will need a lot of creativity, and it will become a much more exciting place to work.

CHANGE DRIVEN BY CONSUMERS

Up until now, change has mostly been technology-driven, a supply push rather than a demand pull. Right now we have the digital revolution, with chips being built into almost all products, the mobile phone, and the Internet revolution. Before that, we had the car industry, and before that we had electricity, steam, and railroads to push growth. The next revolution is about to happen now; the only difference is that this time the driver will not be some new technology, but rather human dreams. It's as forceful as the technological ones or even stronger.

IS THE WEST HEADING TOWARD A REAL REVOLUTION?

A revolution occurs when the established order is overturned by the people—violently or not. Revolutions do happen, and it is likely that we haven't seen the last one. We haven't seen the end of history; it never ends because new ideas and dreams will always emerge, usually unexpectedly, ignited by some book or some event. It won't be Woodstock this time, but some other

spark will unleash a movement—a new dream. Revolutions take time to build up (and it can be long), and then comes the avalanche.

The other possibility is a more evolutionary process. Let's look at three scenarios—all of them are likely, and all of them are about major changes in Western societies and companies. It is the end of business as usual.

First Scenario: The Renaissance Society

The Renaissance in Europe started 600 years ago. It was about setting people free from the iron grip of the church and the king. It was a protest against authority, but it definitely was not a violent revolution. It was created by thousands of young people who by their example led people into a future that was very different from the old hierarchies. It was people with names like Leonardo da Vinci and William Shakespeare, but many others as well, who revolutionized art, science, and geography. It was the end of what is termed the Middle Ages. The Renaissance was about colors, happiness, innovation, and scientific breakthroughs, but mostly it was about the value of individuals, about the right of every person to his own ideas and beliefs.

A second Renaissance in the West must be about nonmaterial values, since 75 percent of GDP comes from services and because we cannot return to materialism. It must be based on the flat society, self-organizing, and decentralization, and the ideas will center around happiness, thriving, and the good life. It will be about the flowering of thousands of ideas and dreams, dreams that are strongly believed in. The result will be new economic growth, nonmaterial growth. When learning and healthcare are the largest growth industries in the world,

we can assume that most innovative ideas will happen within these two industries. Like the first Renaissance, this second Renaissance will be perceived as a threat to established institutions, and it will be. New social heroes will unseat the old ones. The new Renaissance in the West will be about setting people free, like the first one. It will allow dreams to be acted upon.

Second Scenario: The Green Society

We must realize that we have to obey the laws of nature. We must take care of our environment. The globe is a fragile system, and we must preserve it in order to survive. This is an evolution that is happening right now; the road to a sustainable future is the chosen one. It will happen soon or in the long term. We may claim that is a dream, but it is a dream that is believed by more and more people. Often it is a popular movement rather than one fostered by governments and companies. It is a process with many compromises. Is this dream strong enough to reignite the majority?

Third Scenario: The Risk Society

"The Risk Society" is one label that has been given to modern Western society. In one way it is nonsense, since life has never been safer. Never before have so many illnesses been curable; never before has our average lifetime been longer. Never before has it been safer to walk in the city at night. In another sense, however, it is true. The number of rules and regulations imposed to make us healthier has never been higher. We are told that a lot of the things that most of us do every day are dangerous. Actually, we are advised not to do what is enjoyable. Many people try to follow the rules, but it is impossible

to follow all of them. It could be called Puritanism. The old Puritanism was about the healthy soul—the right beliefs. The new Puritanism is concerned not about your soul, but about your body. A healthy body is a good thing, but the impossibility of observing all the rules creates stress and uncertainty. Am I living the right life, am I behaving in accordance with what I have been told? These questions will limit our desire to fulfill our own dreams.

THE EXCITING FUTURE

Will the future be scenario one, two, or three? Or will it be quite different from any of them? We cannot be sure, but the trends outlined in this book suggest that major changes lie ahead. It depends on you more than it has anytime before in history. The changes will not come from the top of society, but from the many—from you and me. Let us meet the future as a friend, not as an enemy.

References

CHAPTER 1

"A Better Measure," *Time*, November 2009.

Steward Brand, *Whole Earth Discipline* (New York: Penguin, 2010).

"Church Attendance by Country," World Values Survey, NationMaster .com, 2010.

Patrick M. Cronin, ed., *Global Strategic Assessment*, "America's Security Role in a Changing World," National Defense University Press.

"Cyberinfrastructure Vision for 21st-Century Discovery," US National Science Foundation, 2007.

"Grand Theft Data," *Financial Times*, April 30/May 1, 2011.

Geert Hofstede, *Cultures and Organizations* (New York: McGraw-Hill, 2010).

"Income, Health, and Wellbeing Around the World," Gallup World Poll, 2008.

"Interpersonal Trust," WVS Archive and ASEP/JDS, 2010.

Rolf Jensen, *The Dream Society* (New York: McGraw-Hill, 1999).

John Maynard Keynes, "Economic Possibilities for Our Grandchildren," in *Essays in Persuasion* (1930; repr. New York: W. W. Norton & Co., 1963).

Angus Maddison, *The World Economy: A Millennial Perspective* (Paris: OECD, 2001).

"Mental Disorders in the USA," Medicinenet.com, 2011.

Nicholas Ostler, *The Last Lingua Franca: English Until the Return of Babel* (New York: Walker & Company, 2010).

Mark Penn with E. Kinney Zalesne, *Microtrends: The Small Forces Behind Tomorrow's Big Changes* (New York: Twelve Books, 2007).

Rolf-Herbert Peters, *The Puma Story* (London: Marshall Cavendish, 2008).

Joseph Pine II and James Gilmore, *The Experience Economy*, Boston: Harvard Business Review Press, 2011.

"Religion in the World at the End of the Millennium," Gallup International, 2000.

Goldman Sachs, "The Exploding World Middle Class," Global Economics Paper No. 170, 2011.

"The Future of Terrorism," *DiscoverMagazine*, July 25, 2006.

"The Global Middle Class," www.pewglobal.org, 2009.

"The Happynomics of Life," *New York Times*, March 12, 2011.

"The Middle Class in India," Deutsche Bank Research, February 2010.

The Triune Mind, a Simplified Model of the Mind," Wikipedia, 2011.

"The U-Bend of Life," *Economist*, December 18, 2010.

"Trust Barometer, Annual Global Opinion Leaders Study," Edelman Editions, 2011.

"World Development Indicators," World Bank, 2010.

www.worldvaluessurvey.org.

CHAPTER 2

"Americans Express Little Trust in CEO's of Large Corporations or Stockbrokers," Gallup, 2002.

Chris Anderson, *The Long Tail* (New York: Hyperion, 2006).

"A Special Report on the Future of the State," *Economist*, March 2011.

"ASEP/JDS Data Bank," Jaime Diez Medrano, Director of WVS Archive and ASEP/JDS, April 2010.

Ori Brafman and Rod A. Beckstrom, *The Starfish and the Spider* (New York: Portfolio, 2006).

"Church Attendance by Country," World Values Survey, www .nationmaster.com, 2010.

"Freedom in the World 2011" (Washington, DC: Freedom House, 2010).

Geert Hofstede, *Cultures and Organizations* (New York: McGraw-Hill, 2010).

"Megacities," *Foreign Policy*, October 2010.

National Bureau of Economic Research, 2008.

"Nurses Top Honesty and Ethics List for 11th Year," Gallup, 2010.

"Power Distance Index," www.ClearlyCultural.com/geert-hofstede, April 2009.

"Religious Identities," The Tomorrow Project, 2006.

"State of the World's Cities 2010/2011," UN-Habitat.

"The Happynomics of Life," *New York Times*, March 12, 2011.

"Trustbarometer, Annual Global Opinion Leaders Study," Edelman, 2011.
"Urban Legends," *Foreign Policy*, September 2010.
"World Development Indicators," World Bank, 2010.

CHAPTER 3

"Civic Engagement Highest in Developed Countries," Gallup, January 2011.
"Dirt Is Good for You," www.sciencefocus.com, January 2011.
"Internet Usage Stats," Internet World Stats, 2010.
"Maslow's Hierarchy of Needs," Wikipedia.
"Over 875 Million Consumers Have Shopped Online," The Nielsen Company, 2008.
"Online Shopping: Selling Becomes Sociable," *Economist*, September 9, 2010.
Coimbatore K. Prahalad and Venkatram Ramaswamy, "Co-Opting Consumer Competence," *Harvard Business Review*, January-February 2000.
Coimbatore K. Prahalad and Venkatram Ramaswamy, "The New Frontier of Experience Innovation," *Sloan Management Review*, Summer 2003.
"Print Me a Stradivarius," *Economist*, February 12, 2011.
"The Printed World," *Economist*, February 12, 2011.
"The Slow Movement," Wikipedia.
"3D Printing Spurs a Manufacturing Revolution," *New York Times*, September 13, 2010.
"Ukraine's Response to the Global Food Crisis," World Bank, May 2008.
"World Development Indicators," World Bank, 2010.
"You Choose," *Economist*, December 18, 2010.

CHAPTER 4

Mika Aaltonen, ed., *Robustness: Anticipatory and Adaptive Human Systems* (Emergent Publications, 2010).
Aristotle, *Poetics* (New York: Penguin Classics, 1998).
Bureau of European Policy Advisors, "Investing in Youth: From Childhood to Adulthood," 2006.
Joseph Campbell, *The Hero with a Thousand Faces* (Princeton, NJ: Princeton University Press, 1949).
"Driving Business Intelligence to New Destinations," IBM Software Business Analytics Publication, 2010.

Michel Foucault, *The Archeology of Knowledge* (New York: Colphon Books, 1976).

Barbara Fredricsson, *Positivity* (New York: Crown Publishers, 2009).

Daniel Goleman, *Emotional Intelligence* (New York: Bantam Books, 1995).

Henry Greely et al, "Towards Responsible Use of Cognitive-Enhancing Drugs by Healthy," *Nature* 456, 2008.

Judith Hortsman, *The Scientific American: Brave New Brain* (Jossey-Bass, 2010).

"IBM Cognos 10: Intelligence Unleashed. Freedom to Make Smarter Decisions That Drive Better Business Results," IBM Software Group white paper, 2010.

William James, *Pragmatism: A New Name for Some Old Ways of Thinking*, 1907.

Ray Kroc and Robert Anderson, *Grinding It Out* (New York: St. Martin's Paperbacks, 1977).

"La CIA au service de Hollywood," *Le Journal de Dimanche*, June 16, 2002.

Jacques Lacan, *Écrits. A Selection.* (New York: W. W. Norton & Co., 1956).

Jacques Lacan, *The Four Fundamental Concepts of Psychoanalysis* (Harmondsworth, UK: Penguin Books, 1979).

John Markoff, "Computer Wins on *Jeopardy!*: Trivial, It's Not," *New York Times*, February 16, 2011.

Robert McKee, *Story* (New York: Regan Books, 1997).

Kathryn Schultz, *Being Wrong: Adventures in the Margin of Error* (Portobello Books, 2010).

Kathryn Schultz, "Making Good Mistakes," *Royal Society of Arts Journal*, Autumn 2010.

Eric Siegel, "Seven Reasons You Need Predictive Analysis Today," *Predictive Impacts Publication*, 2010.

The Book of Zen, Asiapac Books & Educational Aids, 2010.

"The New Idolatry," *Economist*, April 24, 2010.

Paul Virilio, "The Original Accident," *Polity*, 2007.

"WikiLeaks and Julian Paul Assange," *The New Yorker*, 2010.

Ludwig Wittgenstein, *The Blue and Brown Books: Preliminary Studies for the "Philosophical Investigations,"* (New York: Harper and Row, 1958).

"Who Controls the Internet?" *Financial Times*, October 9/19, 2010.

Carl Zimmer, "The Brain: How Google Is Making Us Smarter," *Discover Magazine*, February 2009.

CHAPTER 5

"Algoritmic Trading," www.answers.com.

Chris Anderson, *Free: The Future of a Radical Price* (New York: Hyperion, 2009).

Clement Bezold et al., *"Foresight for Smart Globalization: Accelerating and Enhancing Pro-Poor Development Opportunities,"* e-book, Institute for Alternative Futures and The Rockefeller Foundation Workshop report, Bradford, U.K.: Emerald, 2009.

"Big Society: Radical Ideas from a Frusty Island," *Economist*, March 17, 2011.

"Enemies of Progress. The Biggest Barrier to Public Sector Reform Are the Unions," *Economist*, March 17, 2011.

"Global Risks 2010: A Global Risk Network Report," World Economic Forum, January 2010.

Ray Kurzweil, "Your Future with Robots," sciamdigital.com, 2011.

"Leviathan Stirs Again," *Economist*, January 23, 2010.

Michael S. Loescher et al., *Proteus: Insights from 2020* (New York: Copernicus Institute Press, 2000).

Bernard Mandeville, *The Fable of the Bees* (1705; repr. Harmondsworth, U.K.: Penguin, 1970).

Pravin Palande, "Fat Fingers, Traders and Algorithms," business.in.com, 2010.

J. Palley, "Milliseconds Matter," *Wall Street & Technology*, August 8, 2005.

Johan Rockström et al., "A Safe Operating Space for Humanity," *Nature* 461, September 2009.

"Seven Things You Should Know About Augmented Reality," www.educause.edu/eli

Georg Simmel, *The Philosophy of Money* (London: Routledge & Kegan Paul, 1978).

"Taming Leviathan: How to Slim the State Will Become the Great Political Issue of Our Times," *Economist*, March 17, 2011.

"The Oxford Scenarios: Beyond the Financial Crisis," *The Oxford Scenarios,* Institute for Science, Innovation and Society, Said Business School, James Martin 21st-Century School, University of Oxford, 2010.

"The World's 4-Trillion-Dollar Challenge: Using a System-of-Systems Approach to Build a Smarter Planet," Executive Report, IBM Global Business Services, January 2010.

Bryant Urstadt, "Trading Shares in Milliseconds," *MIT Technology Review*, January/February 2010.

Paul Virilio, *The Original Accident*, Cambridge, U.K.: Polity, 2007.

CHAPTER 6

Mika Aaltonen et al. "Emergence and Immergence of Viruses," *E:CO*, Vol. 12, No. 4, 2010.

Barbara Adam, *Timescapes of Modernity: The Environment and Visible Hazards* (London: Routledge, 1998).

Barbara Adam, *Time* (London: Polity Press, 2004).

Barbara Czarniawska, *Narrating the Organization: Dramas of Institutional Identity* (Chicago: University of Chicago Press, 1997).

Barbara Czarniawska, *Writing Management: Organization Theory as a Literature Genre* (Oxford: Oxford University Press, 1999).

Daniel Goleman, *Emotional Intelligence* (New York: Bantam Books, 1995).

"Google Management Principles," a presentation by Melissa Mayer. http://stanford-online.stanford.edu.

Niklas Luhmann, *Social Systems* (Stanford: Stanford University Press, 1995).

Humberto Maturana and Francisco Varela, *Autopoesis and Cognition* (Boston: Reidel, 1980).

Henry Mintzberg, *Structure in Fives: Designing Effective Organizations* (Englewood Cliffs, NJ: Prentice Hall, 1992).

Friedrich Nietzsche, *Also Sprach Zarathustra: Ein Buch fur Alle und Keinen*, 1883-1891.

Ralph Stacey, *Complex Responsive Processes in Organizations* (San Francisco: Berrett-Koehler, 2001).

"WikiLeaks and Julian Paul Assange," *The New Yorker*, 2010.

Index

About the Authors

Rolf Jensen

Rolf is the author of the bestseller *The Dream Society*. He advises major international companies in many countries, including the United States, Canada, South Korea, and Brazil. He writes and gives presentations to inspire people and companies to change, as change is essential in the new global economy.

Rolf says, "No strategy is better than the view of the future it is based upon." This is especially applicable in a period when the economy is emerging from a severe downturn. It is vital that we leave the "doom and gloom" mentality. That's why *The Renaissance Society* is about new possibilities in management and technology. It is about the new consumer in the mature and in the emerging economies. Rolf and Mika's book is a clarion call for a new logic—a rebirth, a renaissance.

Rolf says, "I hope to convince the business community that high economic growth is possible. Our economies are called 'mature.' We need to become less mature and explore global possibilities, and not just in the short term. Think about 'the extended now.' It is a fantastic source of renewal and growth."

Mika Aaltonen

Mika has a PhD in economics. He is Adjunct Professor of Foresight and Complexity, a member of the editorial board of

E:CO (*Emergence: Complexity and Organizations*) journal and of *European Futures Research Journal*, a Fellow of the Royal Society of Arts in London, Senior Associate Researcher at the London School of Economics, and a faculty member in the master's programme in Foresight and Innovation at the Université d'Angers, France. He is also Head and Chairman of the Board of StraX (the research unit for strategic intelligence and exploration of the future) at Aalto University and the CEO of Helsinki Sustainability Center.

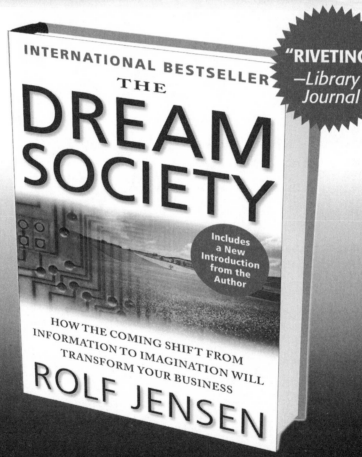

MAY 3 0 2013